AF591213

# MAKING MONEY IN CHILD CARE PHOTOGRAPHY

RICK FONTES

*a comprehensive guide to building your photography business*

Cover Model: Megan Lee Burns
Author Photo: Ruth Fontes

Making Money In Child Care Photography
Third Edition

Published by Lulu.com

ISBN 978-1-257-09730-2

MAKING MONEY IN CHILD CARE PHOTOGRAPHY

TABLE OF CONTENTS

# MAKING MONEY IN CHILD CARE PHOTOGRAPHY

## Introduction

Why child care photography? When faced with the many avenues for expression available to today's photographer why would anyone choose the child care industry as an outlet for his or her photographic effort?

The short answer is - money. No other segment of the photography industry will allow a newcomer to step in and earn on par with the seasoned pro from the very beginning. No other segment of the photography industry offers a return on investment as quickly as does the child care market.

An average child care facility, requiring approximately three hours to photograph, can easily yield gross sales of around $1600. Net revenues will depend on how well the individual photographer is able to control the associated costs but 30% bottom line figures are quite common.

As a general rule, parents of the children attending a child care facility are employed. If it were otherwise they would have no need for child care. Exceptions to this are Mother's Day Out programs and certain government sponsored outreach groups designed to provide opportunity for disadvantaged parents and their children. By and large, however, the parents of your little subjects will be employed and possess the discretionary income needed to purchase your product.

This manual is designed to serve as a workbook, each section addressing a particular area of concern in establishing and operating your child care photography business. Keep in mind that each person using this workbook will be starting from a different perspective. Some will be completely new to the photography business, others will bring years of experience. The information offered must, therefore, be general in nature.

Since each section addresses a different facet of the business, each should be studied as a unit. You may expect some minor overlapping of subject matter from one section to the next. This has been done to provide proper context and make for easier absorption of the material.

I advise you to read the entire manual before you begin to carry out the specific instructions. This will familiarize you with the complete scope and help to avoid delays that can be caused by having to meet unexpected requirements. Once you have completed an initial read through, set your priorities. List the sections in the order that, given your current experience level, seem the most logical and begin.

The equipment used in a child care photography business will vary from person to person as will the amount of energy and dedication brought to the process.

Your geographical location and your financial expectations will play a major roles in how successful you will be operating a business based totally on child care photography. It would be disingenuous of me to claim that a successful child care only business can be operated without regard to the number of facilities available to you.

Urban areas with high concentrations of child care facilities can easily support one or more photography businesses specializing in this market. More sparsely populated areas will require that your child care photography be used as an adjunct to some other form of endeavor.

Projected income figures in this manual are based on nationwide averages for child care enrollment and assume that no more than one facility will be photographed on any given day.

The information I am about to share with you comes from my personal experience, having spent more than thirty years in the child care photography business. While it is never too late to be surprised, I feel that I have encountered just about any situation likely to arise during your child care contacts.

I have hired, trained and supervised hundreds of photographers, sales representatives and support personnel in every section of the United States and the vast majority of those individuals came to this industry with no prior experience. I am confident that, if you complete the simple steps contained in this workbook, you will be able to build a successful child care photography business.

Let's be clear, child care photography is not for everyone. It requires that you be able to work on a child's level when appropriate and switch to an adult, businesslike level when that approach is called for. This is not the career field for the uptight personality. Your adult clientele must recognize your business acumen but the kids have to think you're having fun with them. The highest compliment you will receive from your young subjects is when they say, "you're silly."

The average school will have 40 children enrolled in their full day program. Depending on the number of infants and toddlers present, this average school will take 3 to 4 hours to photograph. This is 3 to 4 hours of nonstop action without a break. To emphasis, this is 3 to 4 hours of intensive involvement with small children, some of whom will not be willing participants in the process. Repeat business will depend, in large part, on the impression you make on the school staff while actually working with the children. This is no fit occupation for 'prima donnas' or those with short fuses.

Most child care directors look upon their facility as an extension of their home. In point of fact, many child care facilities are either in private homes or houses that have been converted to school purposes. You will encounter child care directors who actually live on the premises. It is advised that you act as though you are in someone's home whenever you are photographing in a child care facility. The same rules of courtesy will apply.

Child care directors and their staff will generally offer more help than you need rather than the opposite being true. 'Picture day' is a big event and you will find that most of the staff will be very interested in what you are doing. There will usually be someone at hand to help with any of the little ones who are reluctant to warm up to a stranger.

Use the staff to your advantage. Tell them what you need in the way of space and explain the order in which you will be photographing the children. Generally speaking, the shooting order will be toddlers first followed by the older children in advancing age groups. Infants are photographed whenever they are awake. We will cover this in greater detail in the appropriate section. Shall we begin?

## SECTION ONE

## THE BUSINESS OF DOING BUSINESS

There are certain legal requirements that must be addressed before you start to build your child care photography business. If you already have an established studio, or some other form of registered business entity, you may wish to pursue child care photography as an addition to that business. If, on the other hand, you are establishing a new business you should complete the items in this section prior to moving on to those that are specific to operating the business.

The simplest way to establish your business is to choose a name and register it. You will find an office in your county court house set up to register business names. These are variously known as 'DBA: doing business as', 'assumed names'; or simply 'business names'.

The court house clerk will walk you through the process and there is usually a nominal fee for this service.

If your state has a state sales tax, you will need to contact the taxing authority and get plugged in to the sales tax collection system. The county clerk who registers your business name will be able to point you in the right direction. If not, go online to your state's web site or just look in the government section of your telephone directory.

With the form showing you have registered a business name in hand, your next stop will be the bank to open your business checking account. A minimum deposit may be required and this will vary from bank to bank.

While at the bank inquire about charge card services. You will need to be able to accept credit cards from the parents in the child care facility. There are several companies that offer merchant card services and their fees do vary so, after consulting with your banker, be prepared to shop around before you sign a contract.

Keep in mind that card readers which require a land line telephone connection can not be used in a child care facility. You won't be allowed to tie up their phone service while you are conducting a picture sale. Card readers that use a cell phone connection are usable but be mindful of the minutes charge before you opt for this type of device.

You'll need a supply of business cards. If you are able to design and print these at home then, by all means do so. If not any good office supply store will be able to provide this service to you. The same is true for the other printed material you will need for your business. Among these will be posters to announce your picture day dates and posters to inform the parents when the finished product will be back in the child care facility.

Visit several office supply stores and print shops before making your selection. Ask to see samples of their work and compare the prices. Observe how they treat their customers. Introduce yourself to the store manager and explain that you are setting up a child care photography business and anticipate an ongoing future need for printing services. You will soon get a feel for which of these stores will value you as a customer and be willing to help solve any printing problems that might crop up.

There are several different ways to set up your business entity. Among these are partnerships, corporations and sole proprietorships to mention just three. My personal opinion is that the simpler the better when you are starting a new venture and so I lean toward the sole proprietorship. Each person starting a new business will have to take into account their own unique situation before making this decision but, all things equal, I would start as simply as possible and add to that business model as needed.

Most child care photographers, who are not operating some other business as well, work from their homes. If you elect to office in your home you might want to consider getting a separate mailing address for your child care photography business. Early on in my career I had my home address printed on my business cards and was treated to several unexpected, odd-hours visits from child care parents. A post office box will suffice but you will not be able to receive packages shipped via Fed-Ex or UPS. There are several franchise mail facilities which will provide you with a street address and will accept shipments for you.

If you are not certain which business model you wish to adopt you should talk to friends or relatives who have already been through the process. Lacking this sort of contact, you can always seek advice from your banker.

Other sources for business startup know-how can be found at the U.S. Small Business Administration listed in your telephone directory or by contacting the Service Corps of Retired Executives (SCORE). Both are excellent sources for information.

There are probably a good many accountants or attorneys in your area who will be happy to advise you for a fee. If you choose to contact a professional and pay for the advice you seek, keep in mind that they charge by the hour. Have your questions written down before the meter starts to tick.

Insurance is one area in which you absolutely must contact a professional. You can begin by talking to any agent with whom you currently do business. It doesn't matter the type insurance being provided as you are merely seeking direction at this point. It may be that an umbrella policy can be attached to some existing policy to provide you with liability coverage while operating your business on child care facility property.

Do not attempt to operate a child care photography business without adequate coverage.

## SECTION ONE ACTION CHECKLIST:

*Complete all applicable actions*

1. CHOOSE A NAME FOR YOUR BUSINESS.

2. GO TO YOUR COUNTY COURTHOUSE.

3. REGISTER YOUR BUSINESS NAME WITH THE COUNTY.

4. CONTACT YOUR STATE SALES TAX AUTHORITY.

5. COMPLETE PAPERWORK ALLOWING YOU TO COLLECT STATE SALES TAX.

6. GO TO YOUR BANK.

7. SET UP A CHECKING ACCOUNT FOR YOUR BUSINESS.

8. BEGIN PROCESS TO FIND A MERCHANT ACCOUNT VENDOR AND FOLLOW THROUGH AS APPROPRIATE.

9. VISIT SEVERAL OFFICE SUPPLY STORES AND COPY CENTERS.

10. CHOOSE THE STORE THAT WILL BEST SERVE YOUR NEEDS. ORDER BUSINESS CARDS THROUGH THEM

11. COMPARISON SHOP FOR INSURANCE COVERAGE.

12. SEEK PROFESSIONAL BUSINESS COUNSELING.

13. CHECK WITH US/SBA OR SCORE FOR ADVICE.

14. CONSIDER RENTING A POST OFFICE MAIL BOX OR USING A FRANCHISE MAIL SERVICE FOR YOU BUSINESS ADDRESS.

15. DECIDE WHETHER YOUR TELEPHONE MESSAGING SERVICE IS ADEQUATE FOR THE BUSINESS IMAGE YOU SEEK OR IF YOU WOULD PREFER TO USE A LIVE VOICE ANSWERING SERVICE

"If not now, when? If not me, who?"

# SECTION TWO

## ASSEMBLING A CLIENT LIST

In order to succeed at any business you must know who your clients are and where to find them. For child care photographers this task is far easier than it is in most other types of photography. For the most part the job of identifying and locating your potential clients has been done for you.

Any business that provides child care services must register with a state agency, an exception being certain “in home care” operations which have a very limited number of children enrolled. Generally these facilities are too small to be of interest to you.

State child care listings are a matter of public record and are your's for the asking. While most can be accessed online, the specific pathway to that information will vary from state to state. You can always begin your search by entering “locate child care” followed by the name of your state. In some cases the state child care facility lists will be readily apparent, in others you may have to search a bit deeper but they will be there. As a last resort you can use the yellow pages.

Once you have located the listings you will want to print them. Print each facility's information on a separate page as these will now form the nucleus of your sales calls record system.

The printed listing may be adequate for your record keeping purposes just as it comes off the the printer. This will depend on the format used by your state's child care licensing agency. If not, you will want to create your own form to use for this purpose.

Listed below is the information you will track.

| | |
|---|---|
| SCHOOL NAME | |
| ADDRESS | |
| CITY | COUNTY |
| CONTACT PERSON | TITLE |
| PHONE NUMBER | SALES TAX RATE |
| HOURS | 12 MONTHS Y_ N_ |
| BUS SERVICE | MAP LOCATOR |
| LICENSED CAPACITY | ENROLLMENT |
| HISTORY | |
| HISTORY | |
| HISTORY | |
| PERSON CONTACTED | DATE |
| NOTES | |

If the state's printout has enough space for you to write in the additional information you wish to include, then use it.

The state's list will contain most of the information you will need. At the very least it will have the name of the facility, the address and telephone number. Typically it will also have the name of the registered owner and the number of children the premises is licensed for.

If there is not sufficient room than you will want to create your own form to include space for all the information blanks on the sample above.

Depending on your personal preference, the form can be created on letter-sized paper or index cards.

I am assuming that you have access to a computer. For those who do not, the child care lists are generally available in a printed form from the state agency or can be compiled from the local telephone directory.

Before venturing out to make sales calls you will want to verify the information on the facilities lists. To save time and expense, this will be done by telephone. Your approach will be similar to the following. First introduce yourself, "Hi, I'm Bobby Brown with Happy Tots Photography." State your purpose, "I'm calling to update our computer information on local schools." Clear time conflicts, "Can I take just a minute of your time to ask a couple of questions?"

Start at the top of your information form. Verify the name of the facility, the address, and that you have used the preferred contact telephone number. Ask the director's name, the age range of the children enrolled and the hours of operation. Ask if they are open year round and confirm the number they are licensed to have on the premises. Be sure to ask how many are currently enrolled and what the split is between full day and after-schoolers

"Bus" refers to whether or not the facility provides transportation for any of the children between their homes and the facility and, if so, what percentage. This information will often determine how the photographs will be presented to the parents what sort of payment system can be used.

You do not need to ask about sales tax at this point. Your state taxing authority will provide you with that information and with a breakdown of how the rate might vary from one county or municipality to the next.

Do not short change yourself when gathering information. Time spent here will pay great dividends later when you begin to make personal visits to the child care facilities.

GPS is changing the way we travel but it is not yet a universal tool. The old reliable street finder map will still be your best friend out in the field.

Equip yourself with a high quality street finder that covers all of the area you intend to work. While larger urban areas will require that you purchase two or more street finders, they may not be available at all for rural areas.

If there are no appropriate street finders, you will want to build a collection of fold-out street maps covering all of the area you intend to canvass. These are not as easy to work with while in your vehicle but, if nothing else is available, you must use what you have.

Using your facility's lists, locate the coordinates for each school and enter them as “map locator.” Having this information available will save a lot of time when you are routing your sales calls.

You can’t expect to close a sale each time you visit a child care facility. Over time each sales person will establish a personal average of closings per calls made. My personal average was one child care facility booked for every five calls made.

Your personal average will depend on several factors. Among these are your personality, the amount and quality of competition in the area, the experience that a given facility director has had with other photographers, and the program you are offering, to name just a few.

It may seem unnecessary to mention but you must control the negatives. Dress for success. This doesn't mean that you have to be outfitted like a corporate CEO. Business casual is fine. The rule to keep in mind is that you don't want your appearance to detract from your presentation.

Be prepared. Since you have designed the program that you are presenting, it isn't too much to ask that you be knowledgeable about it. If a director asks a question that you can't answer, say so. Don't try to bluff your way through. All you have to do is promise to get the information requested and then get back to her with it.

A final word on booking averages, once your approach has been polished through use and you become totally comfortable cold-calling directors your personal average will establish itself. From that point forward you will be able to use that number to estimate future income by the number of calls you make.

## SECTION TWO ACTION CHECKLIST

1. GO ONLINE TO YOUR STATE CHILD CARE LICENSING AGENCY OR.

2. LOCATE THE CHILD CARE FACILITIES LISTED IN YOUR TELEPHONE DIRECTORY.

3. CREATE THE CHILD CARE LISTING FORMS YOU WILL USING WHEN CALLING ON THE SCHOOLS.

4. OBTAIN STREET FINDER OR FOLD-OUT MAPS FOR THE ENTIRE AREA YOU WILL BE CANVASSING.

5. CALL THE CHILD CARE FACILITIES TO CONFIRM AND/OR ADD TO THE INFORMATION YOU HAVE OBTAINED.

6. BE SURE TO RECORD THE MAP COORDINATES.

7. CROSS REFERENCE THE STATE'S INFORMATION WITH YOUR LOCAL TELEPHONE DIRECTORY TO MAKE SURE NO SCHOOLS HAVE BEEN LEFT OFF THE LIST.

"You'll never get a second chance
to make a first impression."

## SECTION THREE

## ROUTING YOUR CALLS

You must learn to route your calls properly in order to maximize your booking efficiency while minimizing your expenditure of time, energy and fuel. I realize that it is possible to achieve similar results by using a computer mapping program but there are good and sufficient reasons to learn and practice the old pen and paper method. Computer mapping, while less labor intensive, does not teach discipline, give the benefit of mentally traveling the booking route while in the comfort of your home and will not be there for back-up should you lose the use of your computer.

The old fashioned method is tedious. It requires a certain dedication to task but it is effective and will smooth your journey through the booking calls.

The tools needed for routing your booking calls include a comfortable place to work, a pen or pencil, a legal pad, your maps and a batch of child care facility printouts.

The most efficient way is to group the child care facility printouts by zip code. Refer to your map, select a zip code to be worked then count the number of facilities in that zip code. If the number is fewer than 20 bring in the adjacent zip code as well. 20 planned calls per day is a good working volume for someone learning the art of cold calling child care directors.

As previously discussed, if you are working from printed sheets you should have a separate one for each child care facility. The same holds true if you have decided to use index cards instead. Once you have the schools separated by zip code, look at the "map locator" section on your printouts and batch them according to which section of the map they are located in.

You will be making "calls" and "call backs" using this routing system. The goal here is is to make best use of the time spent calling on child care directors by eliminating needless driving and backtracking.

Look at your map and determine which child care facility is closest to your starting point. Beginning on the first line of your legal pad, write the name of that facility and immediately below it write the directions from your starting point to that facility. Pretend that you are writing directions for someone else to follow, someone without a map.

Skip a line. Select the child care facility that is closest to your first listed call, enter its name and write directions from the first facility to the second. Again, write them as if the person following the directions has no map and is perhaps a bit thick. Repeat this process until you have listed no fewer than 20 schools.

If you are working a sparsely populated area you may find it necessary to cover more than a single town in order to complete a full day's booking calls. If so, be sure to estimate the driving time required and to lower your number of projected calls accordingly. While 20 calls per day is a realistic estimate in an urban area it might not be reasonable in less populated areas.

In the beginning you should route out a week's worth of calls at a time even if you plan to only work the child care photography business part time. Using this routing method is tedious but, as with most things, it becomes much easier with practice.

As you are developing skill in this method of routing you will run into the "oops" factor several times. This is when you have written all the information for a child care facility and then encounter one that should have been included earlier in the rotation. This happens to all of us. Your remedy is to simply make an insert at the appropriate point and then go on with the list. When the list is completed go back and rewrite the entire list correctly.

Did someone say, "you gotta be kidding?" There is no doubt that this is a tedious chore but trust me, it is a lot simpler and less expensive to take time to construct a usable calling route in the comfort of your home than it is to attempt correcting one in the car or finding that you have to back track 10 to 15 miles because you missed a school.

Secondary benefits of this system are that it frees you from having to think about your next move while actively making the calls and, since you have already "driven" the route in your mind, it will seem very familiar to you.

To those of you who might say that it's time for me to come into the 21st century and rely on Map Quest I say, no thanks. As a personal example, I live on a street that has a north and a south component. Whenever anyone follows the Map Quest directions they invariably call and ask how to get unlost. My first words are, "did you pass a sign saying 'dead end' and are now near a brick house with a swimming pool in the front yard?" When they confirm this I can direct them to the street they should be on. Many times a city street will end and then take up again blocks away. The map services often don't take this break in street continuity into account when you are routed. This may be a minor annoyance when getting to a social gathering but when your time equals money, it loses its ability to amuse.

As you make your sales calls you will visit a number of facilities where the director or decision maker is out or “too busy” to talk to you. Determine if that person will be available later in the day and, if so, put that printout into your call back stack.

If you have routed your calls correctly, you will be traveling in one general direction and will be at the far end of your calling area when you have made all the scheduled calls. At this point you reverse direction and begin to make call backs. This will result in your finishing the day in close proximity to where you began.

It is generally a waste of your time to make appointments for visiting child care directors. The backbone of your child care photography business will be the cold calls. Usually when a child care director tells you that you must have an appointment she is really saying, "I don’t want to be bothered.”

If you are asked to make an appointment attempt to set the date then and there. If she is “too busy” to even discuss a future date, thank her for her time and tell her that you will drop by the next time you are in the area to check and see if she is less pressured. Leave your card and any other material you have prepared, place the printout back in your file for a future call in the normal rotation and move on.

The next section discusses methods used in making booking calls.

## SECTION THREE ACTION CHECKLIST

1. ASSEMBLE THE APPROPRIATE TOOLS:
   a. Pen or pencil
   b. Legal pad
   c. Facility information (printouts or index cards).
   d. Street maps.

2. SEPARATE INFORMATION SHEETS BY POSTAL ZIP CODES.

3. SELECT THE FACILITY CLOSEST TO YOUR STARTING POINT.

4. WRITE THE NAME OF THAT FACILITY ON YOUR LEGAL PAD.

5. WRITE THE DIRECTIONS TO THAT FACILITY.

6. SELECT THE FACILITY CLOSEST TO THE FIRST ONE.

7. REPEAT THE LISTING PROCESS UNTIL 20 ARE LISTED.

8. REWRITE THE LIST IF CORRECTIONS ARE NECESSARY.

"no one is going to start each of your days for you with a pep talk, be a self-starter"

## SECTION FOUR

## CALLING ON CHILD CARE FACILITIES

There is only one reason for you to spend time visiting child care facilities and that is to persuade them to let you provide photographic services to the parents of the children enrolled there. On its face this might seem to be an obvious statement but, once you have spoken to a few child care directors, you will understand how easy it is to get side tracked and forget why you are there.

Child care directors and staff don't interact with many adults during the course of their business days and they enjoy having the opportunity to chat with someone on an adult level. While this makes it easy for you to meet with them it also provides many avenues fro distraction. Be friendly and outgoing but remain focused.

Before you step into any child care facility for the first time remind yourself: You will never get a second chance to make a first impression.

You can't know the mind set of every facility director and so it is imperative that you reduce the possible negatives prior to making the call. If you are a smoker be mindful that most are not and make sure you don't have a distinctive tobacco aroma about you. Dress business casual and always enter a room with a smile.

To succeed in this business you must be clean, neat, organized and possess a thorough product knowledge. You must understand all the elements that go to make up a photography session as well as all the steps that follow after the pictures are taken and you must be able to clearly communicate this information to anyone who asks.

Never assume that the director has absorbed all the information you have presented. Learn to tactfully recap the elements of your presentation until you are certain that she has no unanswered questions.

Child care directors are not usually called in advance for appointments. Your booking will be done on a drop in, cold call basis.

With the exception of the large chain facilities, most of your clients will be "mom and pop" operations and, as a general rule, child care directors respond best to a casual, laid back approach.

One of your greatest advantages as an independent child care photography company is your lack of corporate bureaucracy. Play up this angle and it will pay dividends for you. You are the local guy who gives out his home phone number and responds to all calls personally. Should any unforeseen situations arise, you are the problem solver.

This is not to suggest that you need not prepare for your calls. You must know your program, services and prices as well as you know your own name or your spouse's birth date.

We will cover the various aspects of programs and pricing in a later section. This section deals with booking calls and offers tips on how to make them more successful.

Make sure you have the necessary items with you before you enter the child care facility. Your facility print out serves multiple functions. In addition to being a concise compilation of all the information you need to familiarize yourself with the operation, it also serves as an ice breaker. It can provide you with a non-threatening intro into a dialog with the director.

With this sheet in hand you can justify your visit by introducing yourself and saying something like, "Hi, I'm Mary Martin with XYZ photography and I'm in the area updating our computer information on the local centers." This gives you the opportunity to clear any conflicts with the director's time availability without receiving a negative response concerning your photography services.

Always carry samples of your work. If you are new to child care photography and do not yet have samples of your own, photograph your children or those of friends or family. Alternatively, you can borrow samples. Many processing labs will offer samples of typical child portraiture or you might source them from catalogs. Do not, however, pass these off as your own work. Display the samples and present them as typical of what the parents will be shown. As you grow in the business, you will replace these with your own work.

In a following section we will discuss "freebies" and "spiffs." You will need to carry samples or literature concerning these items as well.

In the child care business the director is usually the decision maker. There are exceptions to this rule, especially in the larger facilities. It is always a good idea to ask the director if she will want someone else from her staff to be present when you show your program. It is a waste of time to make a full presentation to anyone other than the person authorized to say yes to you.

If you have determined that the person you are speaking to lacks the authority to close the deal and the person you need to see is not available, be polite, answer any questions you are asked and then move on. Mark the facility as a call back for later in the day or for whenever you will be back in the area and move on.

There are several bits of information you will want to gather from the director. Among these are:

1. Do they have pictures taken at all?
2. How often?
3. Which company do they currently use?
4. What portrait package arrangements do they get?
5. What price ranges are they accustomed to?
6. What is the "turn around time" for the finished product?
7. What does she like most about her current photographer?
8. What would she change about her current photographer?

This information, along with what you already know about the child care facility from your data bank, will tell you how to present your services. Above all, don't interrogate the director. Make polite conversation and show a genuine interest in her business. Parents have come to expect that their child's pictures will be taken at the child care facility. The director will be using someone's services to accomplish this. It is your job to show how your services will will enhance her clients' opinion of her and her school.

Always keep in mind that child care directors do not do business with companies, they do business with people. The hardest booking to get is where the director and her present photographer are on a friendly, first name basis.

Don't let this discourage you. She and her current photographer were once strangers to each other and this friend to friend loyalty will work in your favor once you are established as a school's photographer.

Never speak negatively about the competition. You may know for a fact that the other photographer's quality is low or that their company is slow to honor commitments but keep that information to yourself.

When the competition is mentioned by a director you should always respond with a positive comment. Something like, "Yes, I'm familiar with their work and, as far as I can tell, they are pretty good at what they do." Then sell the differences between what the competition does and what you offer.

Most parents with children in the child care age range will have them photographed three to four times a year. Most child care facilities will have pictures taken only once per year. Your obvious approach is to key in on the discrepancy. This will enable you to get a foot hold into a school that is completely satisfied with their current photographer.

Acknowledge the director's loyalty to her current photographer and point out that it is not your intention to "bump" them. If the facility is having pictures in the Fall, you'll take their Easter or Mother's Day portraits. If they usually have pictures in the Spring, you can offer Thanksgiving or Christmas. If their current guy doesn't do groups, offer to do so.

Your stress is on the idea that you are offering variety. The parents will be taking their children somewhere for the additional portraits each year and, by allowing you to photograph them, the child care facility will be adding to the services they are providing.

We have had a great deal of success offering "family portrait day" on weekends as a fund raiser for the school and we do not hesitate to show up for their special functions such as carnivals and parties.

Presenting yourself as the "new guy on the block" is always effective. Child care operators are entrepreneurs and they respond to the idea of giving someone from the community a hand up. If you use this appeal, you must follow through with excellent service. One miscue and the director will scurry back to the national mega-company that she has been dealing with.

Personalized service wins the day. Being small and independent can be your greatest asset if you use it correctly. Don't hesitate to give out your personal phone number as well as any other business phone line you might be using. The way to do this is to not have it printed on your business cards or any of your literature but, instead, you write it in as an extra courtesy for director with whom you are speaking. This gives the impression that you are doing something special without you having to say so.

Point out that, unlike a large out of state company, you are always near at hand to personally resolve any difficulties that might arise.

If you are also the photographer, say so. Speak glowingly of how much pleasure you derive from working in the child care environment and how special it is to provide such a service in so friendly an atmosphere.

Ask about the director's own kids. Are they enrolled at the facility?. If not, will she be bringing them on picture day? Mention how great it would be to surprise dad with a new photo of her with the kids.

Dealing with the director's children will be brought more into context in a later section. You will also gain a more complete understanding of the products and services you will be offering.

As you make your booking calls, you will encounter a variety of objections. You should welcome these as opportunities to sharpen your people skills and to actually learn more about the business you have chosen.

Let us now get a clear understanding of what objections really are.

Objections are:

1. The right of the customer.
2. Nothing more than requests for more information.
3. Challenges to help you grow in your business.
4. Absolutely no cause for fear.

I have listed a few of the more common objections you will hear and suggested ways to counter them. Please do not use these as a basis for a canned presentation. Strive to keep your own responses as spontaneous as possible. The main reason this listing has been included is to demonstrate that everyone hears pretty much the same things from the directors when making booking calls.

## COMMON OBJECTIONS

| THEY SAY | YOU SAY |
| --- | --- |
| 1. Your prices are too high. | a. You can't really compare our portrait prices with public school picture prices.<br>b. We give the parents an opportunity to buy studio quality portraits without having to go to the studio.<br>c. When compared to studio prices we are very reasonable.<br>d. (depending on the program) there is no obligation to buy and the children still receive their (freebie).<br>e. Our portrait quality is such that we are able to offer a money back guarantee. As far as I know, no one else makes that offer. |
| 2. It's too disruptive | a. That's the beauty of our program. We do 90% of the work without having to involve you or your staff. |
| 3. I don't want to handle money. | a. And I wouldn't ask you to. Let me explain how our program |

| | |
|---|---|
| | handles that aspect. |
| 4. We just had pictures. | (Determine what sort of program)<br>a. I'm sure they were great but that's not the sort of thing we do. (then make your presentation using a different program).<br>b. Surveys show that parents will have their children photographed at least three times per year. Then trial close on a season 6 months into the future. |
| 5. I can't plan that far ahead. | a. That's the beauty of the computer age. We can plug in a date now and let the machine keep track of it. You won't have to give it another thought. And, as the date grows near I'll be reminded to call you to confirm or adjust the date as need be.<br>b. I understand how you feel but I must point out that we'll soon be in the busy season for all photographers. I'd hate for your kids to miss out on (your program). Why don't we just PENCIL in a |

tentative date? That way I can hold the slot open for you.

| | |
|---|---|
| 6. I won't be working here. | a. You'll be doing a service for your replacement. This can be one less thing for the new person to worry about. Of course any date you select now will be subject to the new director's approval. |
| 7. I have to ask the parents. | a. The parents are under no obligation to buy and each child will receive the (freebie) just for participating.<br>b. Based on your knowledge of the facility's future activities schedule, let's PENCIL in a tentative date. That way the parents can approve the program and the date at the same time. I'll leave some literature for you to show when you discuss it with them. |
| 8. We have a photographer. | a. I'm sure that they do a good job or you wouldn't continue to use them (determine what the other company offers) but you owe it to yourself to keep up with what others can |

bring to the parents.

b. what we offer is totally different (explain your program).

c. Parents like to be offered some variety now and then.

d. Give our program a try during your slow season and see if the parents don't respond well to what we offer.

9. My parents can't afford pictures.

a. Many of your parents might never get the chance to have studio quality portraits of their children. We offer ours at truly affordable prices and the parents purchase only what they can afford. We can even tailor a payment plan to fit their budget.

10. Do you pay commissions?

a. If you would prefer a commission instead of the (freebie) I mentioned, it can be arranged.

b. We like to think of our (freebie) program as a form of commission. This program pleases the parents and builds goodwill. The parents regard it as a gift from you rather than coming from the photographer. A few dollars in commissions will soon disappear but the feeling that your parents get from our program will endure for quite a long time.

c. Quality portraits are expensive to produce and we have a very narrow profit margin. We keep our prices as low as possible and pass the savings on to the parents. As a business person I am sure that you understand that, were we to add a commission on top of the (freebie) we are offering, the quality would go down or the prices would have to rise.

d. My prices are as low as I can reasonably offer and still stay in business. If you would like to add something to my pricing schedule or yourself I can have the price list reprinted to include your commission.

11. I don't have the authority.

(determine who has the authority)

| | |
|---|---|
| | a. In case of an absentee owner say to the director, "Since you are involved with the day-to-day operation you would know best when to schedule photography. Why don't we PENCIL in a date that you know will work and then you can present it to the owner. I'll leave a sample of my program for you to show her." |
| | b. If the decision must be made by a board say, "I will be happy to attend the next board meeting and explain the program to everyone at once. Why not PENCIL in a tentative date, one that you know will work best for your schedule, and we can confirm it at the board meeting." |
| 12. What about my after schoolers? | a. We can arrange to be here extra early and photograph them before they go to school or in the afternoon when they return. |
| 13. What about group pictures? | a. We will also take your class room group pictures. |

| | |
|---|---|
| 14. I don't want high pressure sales. | a. Explain that you don't "sell" pictures, you merely display them and let the parents make up their minds.<br>b. Offer a proof or prepaid program in lieu of presenting finished portraits on speculation. |
| 15. I don't trust prepaid programs. | a. Offer a speculative program. |
| 16. What if the parents aren't happy? | a. Offer satisfaction and quality guarantees. |
| 17. We don't do photography here. | a. This objection is non specific. In order to counter it you must first identify it. Ask, "have you ever done portraits?" If no, go on with your presentation. If yes, ask what went wrong and attack that specific objection. |

Again, these are suggested answers to the most common objections. Study them but do not try to make a 'canned' presentation based on them. Booking schools is not a contest of wills, it is merely a pleasant exchange between two business professionals which will, hopefully, result in a mutually beneficial arrangement

When calling on child care facilities the goal is to convey all the information you wish the director to have, to gain all the information you seek to discover and to keep the entire proceedings on a light and friendly note.

You must avoid becoming confrontational. Never argue with a director. You can't win. Even if you prevail in the argument you lose. You miss out on the opportunity to do business in her child care facility.

When you book a child care facility you will have to leave some record with the director. This will be a simple form listing the services you are providing and setting forth what the school will be expected to do. Always include an agreement block on the form you are using. A typical agreement will be worded similar to:

"ABC Photographers will provide (your program) on (date) There is no obligation on the part of (child care name) to guarantee sales amounts or to supply materials for this program. It is understood that (child care name) will provide space for the photographer and will allow the finished portraits to be presented to the parents in accordance with the specific program selected. (today's date)."

Have a signature block for yourself and one for the child care facility's director. Once the form is counter signed, give a copy to the director and keep a copy for your records. While not a binding contract, getting a signature on this form has a similar psychological effect.

When you leave each call you must make a record of what has transpired. Log the information directly onto the printout or index card. Separate the day's call sheets into "booked" and "not booked."

Be sure to enter the information on the schools you have booked into your calendar date log. This must be done immediately after the booking is made to avoid accidentally giving a booked date to another facility during a subsequent call. Complete all paperwork and date log entries before you leave the parking lot of the school you have just called on.

When training a new booker, we would makea few calls togetherand then I would wait in the car and let him or her "fly solo." The idea was to let them try their presentations and be able to go over the results immediately after the call, while the conversation with the director was still fresh in their minds.

If the visit had resulted in a booking, I would ask them to tell me, in their opinion, what cinched the deal. If the answer they had gotten was "no", my first question was, "did you ask for the sale?"

Too often we get wrapped up in our presentation and forget to ask for the sale. We are so brilliant in our discourse that we expect the director to spontaneously agree to our proposal. It doesn't work that way. You must ask for the sale. It's called "closing."

Your entire presentation should consist of a bit of information and a trial close followed by another bit of information and another trial close. This is repeated until you have said all you can say about your products and services and have answered any and all questions the director might have.

It is extremely important that, once you have made the sale, you stop selling. Anything you say after the director has given you a clear buying signal will only serve to make her change her mind. No matter how well crafted your presentation or how much you'd like to share it in its entirety, the director does not need to hear any more after she has signaled her willingness to use your services.

As we have stated previously, you won't sign them all but your attitude should be "someday." Someday, if I continue to call on these schools, I can sign any and all of them no matter what their current reluctance might be.

SAMPLE AGREEMENT FORM

DATE_______________________

SCHOOL_____________________________________________
ADDRESS____________________________________________
CITY___________________________ STATE____ ZIP______
CONTACT PERSON_____________________________________

PROGRAM____________________________________________
___________________________________________________
___________________________________________________

AGREEMENT: (your company name) will provide the above noted program on (date). There is no obligation on the part of (child care name) to supply materials or to guarantee sales amounts for this program. It is understood that (day care name) will provide space for the photographer and will allow proofs or finished portraits to be presented to the parents in accordance with the program selected.

SIGNATURE__________________________________
SIGNATURE__________________________________

NOTES:

## SECTION FOUR ACTION CHECKLIST

1. ASSEMBLE YOUR BOOKING MATERIALS
   a. CHILD CARE PRINTOUTS OR INDEX CARDS.
   b. MAPS.
   c. SAMPLES.
   d. SIGNS, POSTERS OR OTHER HAND OUTS.
   e. PRE-ROUTED CALL LIST.
   f. DATE LOG.
   g. AGREEMENT FORMS.

2. DRIVE TO THE FIRST FACILITY ON YOUR ROUTED LIST.
   a. HAVE THAT FACILITY'S INFORMATION SHEET IN HAND.
   b. HAVE SAMPLES IN HAND.
   c. HAVE DATE LOG IN HAND.
   d. HAVE AGREEMENT FORMS IN HAND.

3. ENTER THE CHILD CARE FACILITY.
   a. LOOK FOR COMPOSITE PICTURES OR OTHER SIGNS OF PROFESSIONAL PHOTOGRAPHY.

4. LOCATE THE DIRECTOR AND BEGIN PRESENTATION.

5. SECURE THE BOOKING.

6. COMPLETE THE AGREEMENT FORM WHILE MAKING CERTAIN THAT THE DIRECTOR UNDERSTANDS THE SEQUENCE OF EVENTS AS THEY WILL UNFOLD.

7. BE SURE THAT THE DIRECTOR KNOWS HOW TO CONTACT YOU SHOULD ANY QUESTIONS ARISE PRIOR TO THE PHOTOGRAPHY DATE.

8. RECORD THE RESULTS OF THE CALL BEFORE YOU LEAVE THE PARKING LOT.

9. IF THE CALL RESULTS IN A CALL BACK FOR LATER THE SAME DAY, NOTE IT AND BEGIN A SEPARATE STACK FOR THAT PURPOSE.

10. DRIVE TO THE NEXT SCHOOL ON THE LIST AND REPEAT THE PROCESS.

11. WHEN YOU ARRIVE AT HOME AT THE CLOSE OF THE BOOKING DAY, COMPLETE ALL RECORDS KEEPING BEFORE MOVING ON TO OTHER TASKS.

12. DOUBLE CHECK THAT ALL YOUR BOOKED SCHOOLS HAVE BEEN ENTERED INTO THE DATE LOG. THIS WILL PREVENT ACCIDENTALLY BOOKING TWO SCHOOLS FOR THE SAME DAY.

13. IF YOU ARE BOOKING FOR TWO OR MORE PHOTOGRAPHERS, USE A SEPARATE DATE LOG FOR EACH OF THEM.

14. IF FOR SOME REASON YOU DID NOT LEAVE MATERIAL AT A BOOKED SCHOOL, ASSEMBLE IT NOW AND SCHEDULE ITS DELIVERY.

"you're either in the parade or you watch the parade."

## SECTION FIVE

## EQUIPMENT

The best equipment for photographing children in the child care market is whichever make or model of equipment you feel most comfortable with. I will not attempt to make value judgments between different photography gear manufacturers. The most anyone can do, given the wide range of equipment available and the great variations in personal taste among photographers, is to point out which types of gear are necessary for the most minimal approach to the field and allow each individual to choose the specific brands that he or she feels will best suit their personal needs.

Before diving into the subject I would like to reminisce for a moment. When I started out in the child care photography business there were no digital cameras. Film was king. The workhorses of the industry were those big, clunky old cameras marketed under the names "Camerz" and "Nord". These were fixed lens SLR's that required you to physically dolly forward and back to change your subject's image size. There were still a few Camerz twin lens cameras in service that required you also test for parallax, the alignment of the viewing lens with the image capturing lens.

The greatest innovation of the time was the development of the Camerz ZII which gave us the zoom lens and freed the photographer from having to move the camera in order to change image sizes.

The films we used most commonly came in 100 foot long rolls and were either 35MM, 46MM or split 70MM. At the close of a day's shooting, the photographer would cut the exposed film off the roll, place it in a can and either deliver or ship it to a processing lab. Several days later a box of proofs or finished prints would turn up at the photographer's shop.

To save time and lab effort, cropping was done in the camera, usually via a set of cropping guide lines installed in the camera's view finder. Most commercial labs offered editing services which gave them the authority to choose, from several on the film, the best of any given pose and that one would be printed.

And then came digital. Digital photography was going to revolutionize the school photography business. No more costly film to buy. You capture your images on a card, transfer them to disc and erase the card for the next shoot. No more giving control of the editing process to some unseen person in a lab, perhaps half a country away. Now you could conveniently load the images into your computer and, with just a few key strokes, choose the exact ones you want to present to your clients.

Digital cameras were less expensive to buy. A Camerz ZII and the associated lights, power packs, film magazines and other assorted pieces of gear, on the used market twenty years ago, would've easily set you back $5000. Today, you can outfit yourself with gently used digital photography equipment to work the child care market for less than half that figure.

I must admit that I was dragged, kicking and screaming, into the

21st century. I rather liked the idea of cutting film after a hard day's slog in the child care and shipping that film off for someone else to deal with. I also didn't like the idea that shooting digitally required more careful attention to lighting because the process is not so forgiving as is film.

Editing your own images is both a blessing and a curse. Someone once said "procrastination is a thief ot time." I would amend to "a computer is the thief of time." The computer offers so many opportunities to play with, and otherwise enhance our images that it takes a certain amount of will power to do a simple edit, select and crop the images you want to print and walk away from them.

Some photographers crop in the camera. This might save a bit of time when you are loading images to be printed but you give away some latitude in tweaking the poses. Depending on the program you are offering, your basic produced unit will probably be the 8X10. The camera yields an image formatted to 8X12 (4X6). If you shoot an image full frame and print it, unedited, as an 8X10 you will lose information top and bottom. Since I now personally edit all my images prior to printing, I tend to shoot loose and retain the option of cropping top, bottom or moving the image side to side.

Let us now discuss specifically what bits of equipment you will be taking into the child care facility. Please keep in mind that we are dealing with minimal equipment here. If you are a seasoned pro you probably already have all the equipment we will cover here and several other items as well.

Speed of operation is a definite factor to be considered. You will be photographing an average of 40 children in a span of 3 to 4 hours. Any decent digital SLR can keep up with this work load but you must be certain that your lights can keep up as well.

There are basically two types of lighting systems that you will encounter in serving this market, the monolight and the power pack/light head combination. Each has its unique attributes and each has its drawbacks.

The monolight is a device that incorporates its power pack in the same case as the light head. This makes it compact, easy to transport and easy to set up. The chief drawback is its weight and the fact that, if one or the other of its main components should malfunction, the entire unit is out of service. If you were to lose either a light head or a power pack, using the separate components arrangement, the other would still be usable.

The other area of concern is in the weight of the monolight. Since the light head and power pack are encased together, the unit weighs significantly more than does a light head by itself. This weight will be perched atop a light stand, typically five or more feet above the floor and is very susceptible to being tipped over. I lost a new monolight, on the first day it was put into service, when two boys ran through my photo area while I was busy setting up a background and collided with the light stand. It crashed to the floor, destroying the monolight. That light went from "brand new" to "beyond economic repair" in the blink of an eye.

Visit your local camera supply store or browse online. You will find several chat rooms where photographers exchange information. Narrow your search to a couple of mono lights and power pack/light head combinations and then chat with people who have used them.

There is no reason to avoid used equipment when you are starting out. The caveat is to purchase them locally if possible or from a reputable dealer who offers some warranty protection.

The minimum equipment needed will include (film):

1. Camera
    a. Long roll, zoom lens and all camera cords.
    b. Film magazine.
    c. Film changing bag.
    d. Film.
2. Tripod W/fully adjustable head.
3. 2 complete light sets
    a. 2 mono lights or
    b. Power pack capable of triggering two light heads.
4. Light stands
    a. One stand for each light.
    b. One stand for the backdrop.
    c. Backlight stand.
5. Extension cord (50 foot minimum)
6. 3 way plug adapter.
7. Duct tape.
8. Background
9. Posing table with or without arm poser.
10. Posing table cover coordinated with the background.
11. Baby blankets, pink, yellow and blue.
12. Assorted toys and small props keyed to the season.
13. Legal pad, black marker and pens.
14. Post photography information pack.

The only thing that will change when shooting digitally is the camera. You will still need all the other items on this list. Keep in mind that this list is for the minimum equipment required. As you progress in your child care photography career you will undoubtedly add to it.

I anticipate that very few people will be opting for a film based business so I will be very brief in my comments concerning that type of image capture. If shooting film you will need a long roll camera . It is possible to shoot with standard 35MM SLR or medium format but the constant need to reload film makes it impractical.

Your first decision will be whether to use 35MM, 46MM or split 70MM. This will influence your camera purchase. You will be limited in your choice of processing labs due to the decreasing number of photographers using long roll film and you will typically have no say in the editing process, choosing which images will be printed.

The advantages to using film are that you have a greater latitude in lighting; film being more forgiving, you save time by avoiding the entire editing process and the cameras can be had at giveaway prices.

Most photographers today feel that the scant advantages of long roll film are far out weighed by its disadvantages.

From this point forward I will be writing with the assumption that you will be using a digital camera. With the exception of the points I have made concerning a film based operation, everything else is pretty much the same.

The booker will determine the background to be used. His or her sample book contains several to choose from. The key thing to remember about backgrounds is to keep them simple. Whether they be of the old masters variety or scenic, they will have to compliment a vast array of clothing styles and colors when the children are posed in front of them.

All the children in a given child care facility will be photographed on the same background. Often someone will ask if you have any other backgrounds. The answer is "No." You can soften the answer by saying something like, "industry surveys show that parents are more interested in great smiles and pleasant expressions than they are in background variety, this background was selected because it compliments a wide range of clothing options."

I have never been kicked out of a child care facility because of a lack of choice in backgrounds.

Occasionally we offer two different backgrounds in the same school. This is done to solve a problem on our part rather than to give the school a wider choice. When shooting a large school, 80 or more enrolled, you have to decide whether to photograph on two or more days, depending on total enrollment or bring in an extra photographer on picture day. We usually elect to use the extra photographer. This entails two backgrounds and, since we don't normally have two matching backgrounds, we book it as two seasonally appropriate backgrounds, adding to the variety and value of the finished product.

Your total equipment package must be highly portable. You will be taking this equipment in and out of several schools each week. A well designed set of equipment should fit into just about anything you would care to drive. I worked a season out of my '76 VW bug with little difficulty.

Whether you are using mono lights or a power pack/light head combination, you should purchase the manufacturer's carrying case designed for that unit. If you are buying used, then you will want to find a case that carries the light set up, in a padded environment, as snugly as possible.

Some photographers prefer to use a two front light system. Some prefer one key light and one background light. I have a friend who uses a four light system, one key, one fill, one background and one hair light. I must say it looks very professional but does tend to clutter the area and space is at a premium in most child care facilities.

Test the different lighting set ups for yourself and you will soon form a preference. Do remain flexible because there will be times when your preferred method won't be practical and you will have to fall back onto one of the others.

I prefer the single front light, single background light combination in the child care environment because you will always have someone from the staff attempting to help you coax those smiles. If you are using two front lights, one to either side of the camera, your helper will invariably block one of the lights, throwing a shadow across your subject. For this reason I prefer one key light, directly above the camera and a single backlight erasing shadows from the background. If you prefer the two front light system you will be constantly reminding people to not block the light.

When selecting a tripod, err on the side of stability. It is not possible to have too sturdy of a tripod but the opposite is certainly true. Your camera represents a major investment and you will want to protect it by having it attached to the most secure mount you can afford.

Tripod heads are also an important consideration. Be sure the tripod head you select will allow you to shoot in portrait configuration, attaches easily to the tripod and is not prone to slippage.

Posing tables must be lightweight, sturdy and portable. I have built my own posing tables and I have used tables purchased from a major warehouse discount store. While your average subject will be well under 100 pounds, it is to your advantage to have a posing table that will support the weight of an adult. Occasionally you will have an assistant perched on the edge of the table, helping to "jolly up" a reluctant child. You want your table to be able to support that person's weight.

The posing table need not be more than five feet long, a standard size available at discount stores. Your posing table should be about 24 inches from the floor so purchase a table with adjustable legs or be prepared to shorten them.

Arm posers are useful but not indispensable. Sourcing these is covered later.

Backgrounds are an important element in child care photography. A background can range from something as simple as a pastel colored sheet draped over a clothesline to an elaborate MGM type set. We will address the subject with cost and portability in mind. Typically you will have only one background with you when you set up your equipment for a shoot. This particular background will be the one mutually chosen by the director and the booker.

Backgrounds can be purchased from a local photo supply stores, background manufacturers, other photographers or even from online sellers such as ebay. Major background suppliers advertise in photography magazines and most have web sites where you can order their catalogs. Several of our backgrounds were painted by a local artist.

There is no need to go overboard on purchasing backgrounds. A couple of pastel "old masters", and an interior Christmas scene will do nicely for your first year's shooting. As you grow in the business you can invest in a greater variety of backgrounds.

A word of caution, when shooting a Christmas scene be

prepared to change to some other, non religious background, in case you encounter a child whose parents do not observe the holiday. This is something that will have been discussed between the booker and the director at the time it was decided to use the holiday theme and it is up to the school to notify you should a particular child's parent not want the Christmas scene.

Props are highly subjective. The thing to avoid here is "ET's closet." Those of you who remember the movie E.T., will recall the scene in which the alien is hiding in a closet and the space is so crammed with toys that he is not noticeable. Too many toys and your posing table becomes "ET's closet."

While tasteful, age appropriate, toys have their place in your portraiture, they should not dominate the scene. More on this in the next section, "posing."

Backgrounds must be supported on something. We use stands designed for this purpose. A background stand can be exactly the same type stand used to support your lights but it does not have to be. The difference here is that a background stand need not be as sturdy as is the light stand. If you need to shave a few dollars off your start up costs, here is a place to do it.

Commercial baby posers are very expensive pieces of foam that have been especially designed and cut to hold an infant while allowing someone to insert an arm from one side or the other and hold the infant's clothing, preventing the child from tumbling out. They are extremely useful and, as I mentioned, expensive.

Many photographers simply make do with an infant's seat covered by a blanket or by having an assistant drape a blanket over their arm and lean the infant back against their hand. A tummy pose is always a safe bet if the infant can hold his or her head up.

Have a noise maker of some sort. A squeaky toy or a rattle is essential for getting the attention of some infants and toddlers. The best source I've found for squeaky toys is the pet department of the local discount store.

When it comes to toys and props, I am not a great believer in taking pictures cluttered with lots of little cutesy gadgets. My preference is to go for the child's expression and use age appropriate poses. While this is a matter of personal opinion, and I would not quarrel with anyone who feels differently, in the final analysis it is the parents who determine what is or isn't a good portrait. They make this determination with their checkbooks.

You must have a good supply of toys and props and learn to use them judiciously. Toys are an important asset in keeping the younger children amused while they are being photographed. Keep up with the trends among your young subjects and be conversant with the latest trends in cartoon heroes.

Be certain you have a supply of balls, tennis, nerf, super, or whatever. An impromptu game of catch has coached many a grumpy toddler into smiling.

Bubbles are a touchy subject. While they are a sure fire ice breaker for most kids, some directors get really upset when faced with the mess that they can leave behind. Get permission before blowing bubbles. I always tape the liquid container to a leg of my tripod to eliminate the possibility of a major spill.

And now for the most important decision you will have to make, the camera. This subject could easily fill a book of its own but we will attempt to cut to the chase and simplify it as much as possible.

Assuming that you are opting for a digital based photography business, let's discuss the bare necessities when it comes to camera selection. As previously mentioned, I was brought reluctantly to the use of the digital camera. The increasing level of difficulty in finding a long roll film processor who could consistently deliver the quality wanted for my clients, coupled with lessened availability and higher costs for professional grade, long roll film, forced me to make the switch.

After researching the available cameras within my price range I settled on the Nikon D70. As of this writing, we have been using a pair of these in the field for over four years and they have been trouble free.

This camera does have one major flaw when it comes to using it in child care photography and that is the lack of a remote shutter release cable. I thought that we had addressed this when, doing our due diligence, we learned that the camera supported an infrared remote shutter control.

It is very important that you be able to be physically close to the child you are photographing. You have to interact personally with your subject, especially the younger ones, and this is difficult to do when you are standing near the camera.

All of the film cameras I have used over the years were equipped with a shutter release cable five to six feet in length. This allowed you to get up close and personal with the children and heightened the sense that it was all fun and games.

I thought that the infrared feature of the D70 would serve the same purpose and, indeed it does in the landscape orientation. Child care photography, however, is done in the portrait mode. Except for a limited range, the lens tends to block the path to the infrared sensor rendering it ineffective.

Radio slaves are available but, being electronic gadgets, they are prone to failure. Some of the kids are hard to work with and Murphy's law dictates that the radio slave will malfunction at the precise moment that you get the one and only smile from an otherwise crying kid.

The D70 has been an excellent workhorse and, as I said before, it has never stumbled once during a shoot, but we have fought this shutter release problem since day one and, now that the camera's useful life is nearing an end, we will definitely replace it with a camera, without regard to manufacturer, that offers a shutter cable. I very much prefer the simplicity of a direct mechanical link.

This D70 is a 6 mega pixel camera and the image quality has been superb. You will probably purchase a camera with greater resolution but I would definitely not go any lower.

The most important thing to keep in mind is that your camera and your lighting system are a team. Just as you wouldn't assemble a baseball team and put a professional hockey player on the mound, you want to make sure that the components of your equipment team are playing the same game.

When you set out to purchase equipment, look at it as a cohesive unit. The camera, the lights, the power packs, the cabling, all parts of a single package. A reputable photographic equipment store, one that sells both new and used items, is a valuable asset. If you have one within driving distance by all means visit with them and spend time learning how the various components of the system you wish to assemble compliment each other.

If there is no such store near you then go online and find a photographer's chat room. You don't need a lot of esoteric knowledge to ask the correct questions and receive usable information. Basically the elements of your request for information concerning a camera purchase are these.

1. I am going to be shooting pictures in child care facilities.
2. I need to purchase a camera and a compatible set of lights.
3. If mono lights, I need at least one capable of being powered down far enough to be used as a back light.
4. If power pack/light head combo,I need a power pack that will support at least two heads, one of which can be powered down to use as a back light.
5. I need the shortest lighting recycle time consistent with my budget.
6. Some older child care facilities have electrical circuitry that fluctuates when equipment such as AC units or ovens are turned on or off. My lighting system must be able to adjust to any such fluctuations.
7 I need a full set of cables and a full set of spare cables.
8. I would prefer a camera that has a physical remote shutter release and a release cable no less than five feet in length.

if you cover all these points and incorporate them into the final camera and lights package, you will be adequately prepared to shoot in the child care market.

## SECTION FIVE ACTION CHECKLIST

1. VISIT PHOTOGRAPHY SUPPLY STORES AND CHECK OUT WHAT IS AVAILABLE IN NEW AND USED EQUIPMENT.

2. GO ONLINE AND VISIT PHOTOGRAPHER'S CHAT ROOMS.

3. PURCHASE SEVERAL PHOTOGRAPHY MAGAZINES, BROWSE THE ADS AND SEND FOR CATALOGS.

4. VISIT SEVERAL LOCAL PROCESSING LABS AND SEE WHAT SERVICES THEY OFFER. DON'T OVERLOOK THOSE LOCATED IN THE MEMBERSHIP WAREHOUSE STORES.

5. OBTAIN THE FOLLOWING EQUIPMENT:
    a. CAMERA WITH REMOTE SHUTTER CAPABILITY.
    b. MEMORY CARDS.
    c. CAMERA TRIPOD AND FULLY ADJUSTABLE HEAD.
    d. MONO LIGHTS OR POWER PACK W/ LIGHT HEADS.
    e. CORDS, 2 SETS.
    f. POSING TABLE.
    g. ARM POSER (OPTIONAL).
    h. BACKGROUNDS.
    i. LIGHT STANDS AND BACKGROUND STAND.
    j. TOYS AND PROPS.
    k. A SECOND CAMERA FOR GROUPS (OPTIONAL).

"there are no office hours for winners"

## SECTION SIX

## POSING AND SHOOTING

During two decades spent training photographers for a major child care photography company one truth continually showed itself; there is no "correct" way to pose a child. The only proper pose is the one a parent will buy. Your only reason to photograph the children is so that you can provide finished portraits to the parents which will inspire them to reach for their checkbooks.

Your personal opinion of what constitutes a good pose must always be secondary to that of the parent. If you photograph in 100 child care facilities per year, averaging 40 children each, you will deal with 4000 sets of parents. Your challenge is to use poses that will be deemed desirable by a majority of those parents.

With this in mind, let's discuss how to get started posing children in the child care market.

The first thing to consider is how many poses are you going to offer. Programs vary from photographer to photographer and from school to school. Some favor shooting only one pose, some two and some three or more. The posing package that I used for most of my career consisted of three separate poses for each individual child. When there were siblings present in the school, I would shoot one pose of each individual and one pose of them together.

In a three pose mix there will be two close up and one full body or two full body and one close up. The important thing to remember is that you must physically move the child between poses so that you are adding variety. Please resist the temptation to “alter” a pose with the zoom lens. Often a photographer will attempt to fudge by shooting a full body pose, then zoom in for a close up and call that a second pose. This shows a lack of creativity and will have a negative effect on your sales.

It is acceptable to shoot different numbers of poses in different schools but you should standardize the number of poses used in any one facility. This avoids confusion when you are presenting the final product.

Your price lists will be created with a certain number of poses listed. Standardization of your poses helps to decrease the work involved in designing your sales and pricing material.

I teach six basic poses when working with inexperienced photographers. Three are “girl poses” and three are “boy poses.” You will find illustrations of these poses below. Please note that the variations from boy to girl are very subtle. The girl poses merely entail repositioning the hands or legs to soften the image a bit.

As with many aspects of life, the simpler approach is often the better approach. Don’t try to become an instant creative genius when posing the children. Concentrate on learning to work with them and gain their cooperation. If you supply the parents with solid, well framed and sharply focused images of their children, they will reward you with a better than average income. The basics will always sell. After all, the most popular flavor in ice cream is still plain vanilla.

The nine poses on the next page represent a minimalist approach to the subject of what to do with the children once they are on the posing table. While these examples will create pleasant, time-tested images, you are really only limited by your imagination.

Some of these poses require the use of an arm poser. There are several arm poser designs on the market or you can easily construct your own by researching them online and copying what you find. The key, as with all child care photography equipment, is portability.

I am including a URL for those readers who are interested in seeing examples of the poses and backgrounds we are currently using in the child care market. Please keep in mind that conditions change and so, by the time you read this, the site may no longer be valid. To address that possibility I am including my personal contact information in the final section of this manual.

At the present time you may access sample images at:

http://www.viewyourphoto.com/childcare

Please contact me If this site is no longer valid and I will give you an alternate place to view posing samples.

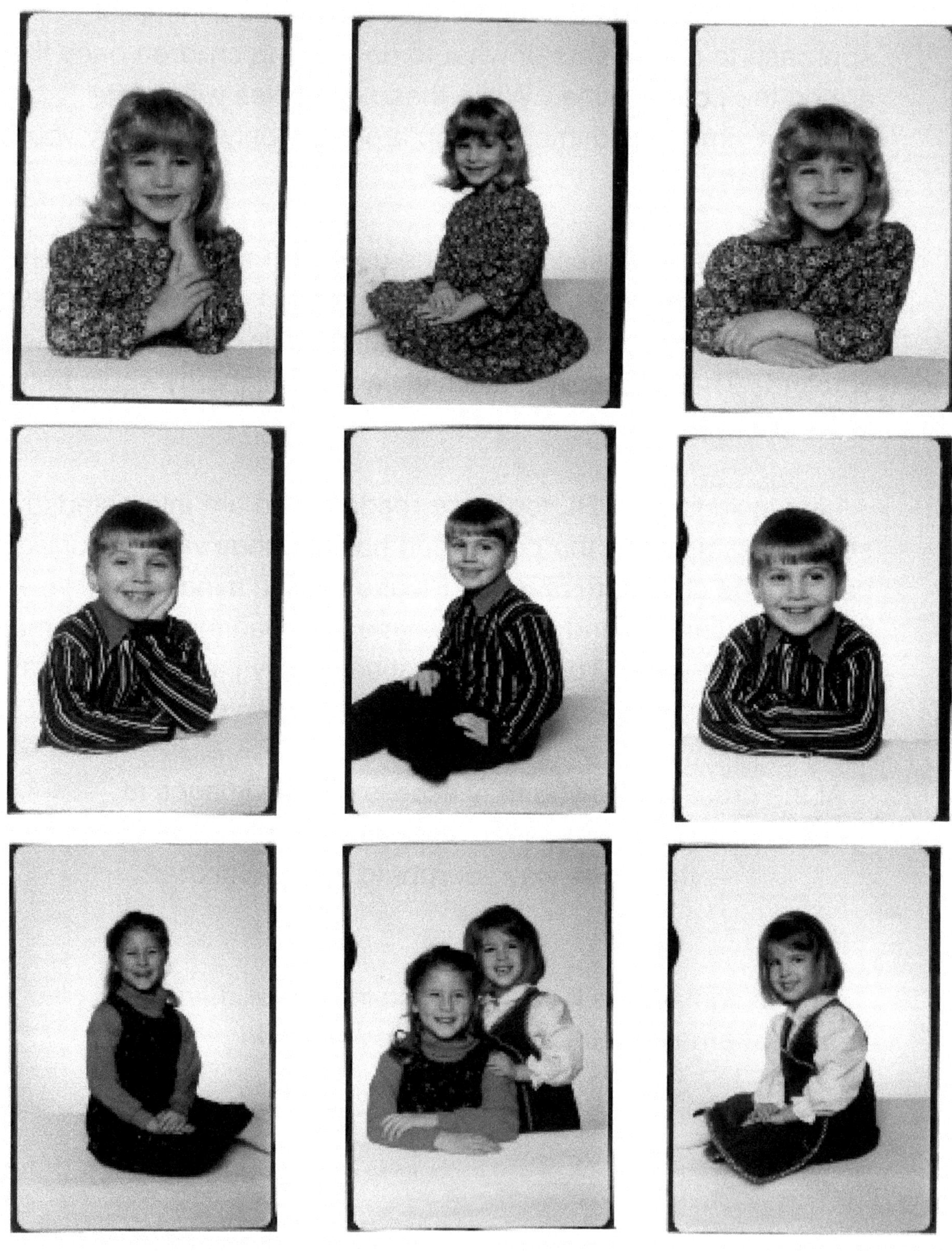

We will now turn our attention to the subject of shooting and posing as a whole.

"Picture day" has arrived. The booker's job has been done correctly, the parents have been notified, the staff is eager and the children have all been scrubbed up and are waiting in their best attire. It is now time for you, the photographer, to work your magic. The success of the entire enterprise now depends on the quality of those images you will capture in the next few hours. So, let the show begin.

The booker will have left some sort of poster announcing the photographer's starting time. Plan to arrive no less than thirty minutes prior to the posted time. The director and the school staff will be expecting actual photography to begin at the posted time. Also, there may be parents who have arranged their day so that they can be present to watch their child's picture being taken. You must arrive early so that you will be able to set up your equipment and be ready to start the shoot on time.

Upon arrival at the child care, immediately locate the director or the person in charge and ask to be shown the room where you will be working. If there is a problem with the space they have allocated, say so.

A good booker will have already covered this with the director but sometimes the needs of the facility will have changed and the space shown to the booker will be different from the one the photographer is taken to.

In order to properly do your job as a photographer you must have adequate space for your equipment, electricity for your camera and lights and sufficient room for the children and staff who will be in the room while photography is taking place.

Discuss the order in which the children will be photographed. Generally you will start with the toddlers because they are the hardest group to work with. While the toddlers will represent only a small percentage of the children enrolled, the bulk of your time shooting will be spent with this group.

After the toddlers you will photograph the older children in ascending age groups, working infants in whenever they are awake and calm.

Most programs will offer to photograph sibling groups individually and together. The way to approach this is to have the older sibling brought to the camera while the younger sibling's class is being photographed. As mentioned, toddlers are your most difficult group and you want to avoid making a toddler wait for his or her older sibling's class to come to the camera.

Keep the area around your posing table and between the table and camera as clear as possible. Any props to be used should be placed within convenient reach, on the floor, on one side of the posing table.

Use duct tape to cover any exposed cords running from your equipment to the wall outlets.

Keep a supply of wet wipes and tissue handy and have a supply of combs. Please remember that combs can be used only once. Nothing will draw the wrath of a director or her staff quicker than seeing you use the same comb on two or more children. Be sure to toss the comb after it is used.

Most child care photographers work alone. The only time you will need assistance is when you are dealing with the smaller children and the person who brings them to you will always remain in the room until you are finished with them. Generally you will not have to ask this person to assist, she will volunteer. All child care workers feel that they can get better smiles from the children than can the photographer and they are always ready to prove it.

Station the child care worker close to the posing table when working with the younger tykes as it can be a long way to the floor for an infant. I usually direct the care giver by saying, "You are the safety control officer. Your job is to see that the baby stays on the table."

No matter which set of equipment you have elected to use, you will be at a disadvantage if you don't have a shutter release cord or some other dependable remote shutter release mechanism.

A shutter release cord should be long enough to allow you to move from the camera to the posing table with ease. The younger children do not respond well to someone who keeps his distance. You have to be close to them in order to make them feel that it's all a game.

If someone from the staff is helping to groom the children they must be told where to stand. The natural position seems to always be between the subject and the camera which prevents you from framing the subject until the grooming process is completed. Ask this person to work slightly to one side so that you can check the child through the viewfinder and make any necessary adjustments while the noses are being wiped.

If you expect to consistently finish your shoots in the time allotted for them, you will have to develop a skill for shaving seconds whenever possible without sacrificing quality.

A word of caution about using ladders, rocking chairs or similar props; they are potentially hazardous. Make sure they are secure. My rocking chairs all have shims affixed to the runners so that they can't rock.

When using any prop be quick to notice if it is making the child uneasy. Different children will react differently to your toys and you must be prepared to immediately remove any that cause an adverse reaction.

Have fun. Where else can an adult spend the day playing with children and get paid to do it.

The best case will be to have several children in the room at the same time. This gives you the opportunity to observe their reactions and to skip over the reluctant ones until they have seen the others in front of the camera. Once the group of children have entered the room, and are settled in chairs or on the floor, you can spend a few minutes "playing" with them as a group. High five's or tossing a ball can be useful diversions which help to get them to lower their guard and will allow you to determine which children will be the easiest to work with.

Play to your audience. While you are working with the subject on the table interact also with the kids on the sidelines. Keep them all involved and active and, when their turn comes they will be happy to jump up onto the posing table.

Grooming and posture are the photographer's responsibility. Develop an eye for detail. Are the shirt's collar points straight? Does the little lady's dress flow smoothly? Are sleeves positioned evenly?

Noses must be wiped, hair combed, snack remnants removed from around the mouth, stickers removed from hands and arms.

Poor posture will destroy the lines of any composition. Position the children correctly and help them to maintain their posture by repositioning them as needed.

In training I use the acronym, "PEP." It stands for the three most important elements of any child's portrait:

POSTURE. EXPRESSION. POSE.

Posture, expression and pose in that precise order. Of these three elements only one is not subjective. While we may disagree on whether a given expression is pleasant or a particular pose is charming, everyone recognizes poor posture.

Shoot the number of poses required for the program you are bringing into this facility. Always shoot at least one extra frame of each pose even if you are certain that you nailed it on the first take. A blink of your subject's eye can slip by unnoticed so you want to have that extra frame for insurance.

Depending on the program, you may or not be using run sheets. A run sheet is a list of the children's names, in the order that they are photographed. The run sheet is compiled as you are photographing the children. Their names are added to the sheet just before, during or just after their turn on the posing table. Many child care facilities will provide a class roster and, in this case, you need only place a number beside the child's name as they are photographed.

Most child care photographers offer to photograph the school's staff. Generally one pose will do. The best time to photograph a staff member is when she is at the camera with her class. If you wait until the end, the staff member will be required to find someone to stay with their kids while she returns to the camera. This can really slow the proceedings. Staff portraits are usually framed as head shots.

All children are equal but the director's children are more equal. If the director has made special arrangements to have her own children photographed, give them preferential treatment.

On the other hand, if the director's children are enrolled at the center, let them come to the camera with their class.

Check with the director before you begin to pack up your equipment. It is also a good idea to pop your head into each classroom and confirm that all the kids have been to the camera. A run sheet, if you are using one, is a major aid in determining that all the children have been photographed.

The school may require you to shoot class room group pictures while you are on the premises for the portrait shoot. If you have a second camera, and if the children have been brought to you as an entire class, then you might consider doing the groups as soon as you finish the individuals.

Lacking a second camera, you would be required to dismount your primary camera from its tripod and disconnect it from the strobes in order to pose and shoot the groups. Since the group shots might also entail changing camera settings, it could affect the quality of your overall shoot when you remount the camera for the next set of individual portraits. I would strongly suggest that you not do this.

If you have a second camera, and if the weather permits, you might consider having the classes go out to the playground for their group shots. This will eliminate the need for added lighting and you can zip out, shoot the groups and be back inside as the next class is coming in for their individual shots.

For inside groups you will need strobes or a good camera mounted flash and a space large enough to line them up in rows, using the facility's chairs for seating. Infant groups are usually photographed in the infant room.

If you must use the same camera for individuals and groups, explain to the director that the groups will have to wait until all the children have had their individual portraits taken.

There are several ways to line up your classroom groups. Here is an extremely simple method. If you have 6 or fewer children, place them in one row of chairs. 7 to 11 children, place half in chairs and the other half sitting cross legged, in front of the seated row. 12 or more, divide by 3 and pose them with one row seated, one row cross legged on the floor and the other row standing behind the chairs.

When posing staff members with the class room groups please watch their height. It ruins the composition if there is too much space between the tops of the children's heads and those of the adults. Have the adults seated, slightly behind the children, or kneeling so that you have a tighter composition, top to bottom.

Complete any paperwork before dismantling your equipment. This allows time for any stragglers to arrive. If you are using individual notification cards for the parents or providing a poster stating when the finished portraits will be back, now is the time to meet with the director and hand them over. Make sure the director has your contact number in case she needs to talk to you prior to when the pictures are returned.

Your equipment will be packed for transport in the same manner each time. This means that you will have a fixed number of cases, bags or what have you. Lay them out on the floor and physically count them before anything is moved to the car. Do this religiously even though you are confident that you will never leave anything behind. Experience has taught me that it is no fun to discover the following morning, that your background is still leaning on a wall, in a school fifty some miles away.

## SECTION SIX ACTION CHECKLIST

1. OBTAIN A STURDY POSING TABLE.

2. OBTAIN ADDITIONAL POSING EQUIPMENT:
   a. ARM POSER (OPTIONAL).
   b. BABY POSER (OPTIONAL).
   c. SOAP BUBBLES (OPTIONAL).
   d. TOY SELECTION INCLUDING SQUEAKS AND RATTLES.
   e. SEVERAL VARIOUS SIZED BALLS.
   f. BABY BLANKETS, YELLOW , PINK, BLUE.
   g. WET WIPES, KLEENEX, COMBS

3. GO ONLINE, STUDY POSES BY OTHER PHOTOGRAPHERS.

4. SELECT A BASIC SET OF THREE OR FOUR POSES AND PRACTICE THEM.
   a. WITH SIBLINGS IT IS IMPORTANT TO "MATCH" THEIR POSES. IF YOU DO A FULL LENGTH WITH ONE, DO A FULL LENGTH WITH THE OTHER, ETC.

5. ARRIVE AT THE CHILD CARE FACILITY NO LESS THAN THIRTY MINUTES PRIOR TO THE POSTED START TIME.

6. SET UP AND TEST YOUR EQUIPMENT.

7. FIND THE PERSON IN CHARGE AND DISCUSS THE ORDER IN WHICH THE CHILDREN WILL BE PHOTOGRAPHED.

8. SPEND TIME INTERACTING WITH THE CHILDREN TO MAKE IT A FUN EXPERIENCE.

9. PAY ATTENTION TO GROOMING AND CLEANLINESS.

10. COMPLETE ALL PAPERWORK.

11. CHECK FOR STRAGGLERS.

12. HAND ALL REQUIRED MATERIAL TO THE DIRECTOR.

13. COUNT AND REMOVE YOUR EQUIPMENT.

14. THANK THE DIRECTOR AND HER STAFF.

“practice. only the mediocre are always at their best”

# SECTION SEVEN

## PORTRAIT PACKAGING AND PRICING

This section will explore different packaging arrangements and help you decide which you want to offer. It will also discuss pricing, premiums, gifts and commissions to the child care facility. We will describe prepaid, proof, and speculative programs and how to handle reorders. Forms and printed materials needed to support these subjects will be covered in the next section.

There are three common methods of presenting the fruit of your labors to the final consumer. They are:

1. Speculative Photography
2. Proof Programs
3. Prepaid Programs

Speculative Photography refers to a method of presentation in which you print entire finished packages for each child photographed. If you elect to use speculative photography, you will need to arrange a date and time to bring the finished portraits back into the school and you will meet personally with each of the parents to show them their child's package of pictures. This is usually done in the afternoon, during the period of time that the parents are picking up their children. A typical portrait showing session will begin around three in the afternoon and last until the facility closes.

Speculative programs require a degree of preparation. You will need a credit card reader or mechanical "swiper", a cash box with change and small bills, pens and price lists.

A poster, generally left by the photographer, announcing the day that pictures are in the school, should have been placed on or near the main entrance. The person who booked the school will have already discussed the space needed to present the portraits. The room must be large enough to accommodate a dozen or so parents at any given time. The school's lunch room is usually the best place for this activity.

Portraits are presented either as packages or priced by the sheet. A sheet is an 8X10 sized print which can contain either an 8X10 or some combination such as a 5X7 and wallets or a 5X7 and 3X5's. Or It can be all wallets.

Package pricing refers to a given number of sheets, which must be purchased as a unit, for a set price. Sheet pricing allows the customer to select any individual sheet or sheets from the set.

The simplest way to distribute the portraits is to have them separated by class or age group, each group in an individual container. If you have the children's name from the photographer's run sheet, you might take the extra step of alphabetizing them.

Price lists will have been placed on the table around the room. When a parent arrives, she merely goes to the container holding her child's group, retrieves the proper package and moves to one of the tables to view them.

As the parents view their child's portraits, the sales people circulate through the room answering questions and assisting in making selections.

When a parent makes a buying decision, the sales person writes a receipt and collects the payment.

At this point we need to discuss some general information on speculative photography programs. Speculative programs are the most risky, financially speaking. They require you to pay all the processing costs before any money changes hands at the child care facility. If the school has the average 40 kids and you are using a three pose, two sheet program, you will have paid to print 240 8X10 sheets, plus any extras for the director and staff. You could easily have $400 invested just in production costs, before the parents ever see the pictures.

The next bitter pill to swallow is that, on average, you will throw away half of what you have printed.

That said, you are probably wondering why anyone would use the speculative method to present portrait packages. The reason is, that of the three most common methods, 'spec' yields the highest dollar returns on investment, even when taking into account the prints tossed away.

A rule of thumb is that your sales average will equal 50% of your full package sales price. If an individual full package sells for $80, your average for the school will be about $40 per package shown.

Speculative selling relies on the maternal instinct and on

impulse buying pressured by the abbreviated time allowed for viewing. While there are definitely opportunities for a loss, this method remains, year in and year out, the most lucrative.

Once all the parents have come and gone you will probably have a number of packages that were not viewed. This is so because some of children will be absent on any given day and because some parents will have taken their children home early. These parents must also be given the opportunity to add to your bank account. You have several ways to approach this situation.

Leaving the packages with the director is probably the most efficient way to deal with unshown portraits. In most cases the director will suggest this if you merely let her know that you have some unshown portraits and, "Oh dear me, what ever shall I do with them?" The director will usually ask if you will trust her to show the pictures and collect your sales. The key is to make it easy for her to collect. We leave a price list in each package. The price list has a complete listing of the purchase prices, by the sheet, and has a space for credit purchasers to write in their account information.

Alternative methods are that you can leave proofs instead of the actual packages and fill orders by mail or you can use one of the on line portrait companies that will fill orders for you, for a fee.

Do not lower your prices in an attempt to move unsold portraits. Yes, they represent a cash outlay and yes, it would be nice to recoup those costs rather than being faced with the prospect of discarding the images, but keep in mind that a major part of what we are doing is educating the customer about the value of our services. If, after a speculative sale, you lower the the price of the unsold images you will, in effect, be educating your customers to wait for the 'fire sale'.

If the portraits aren't purchased at your posted prices, bite the bullet and destroy them.

Proof Programs generally yield lower total dollar amounts, in a given school, than do speculative programs. Its chief advantage is that you aren't paying production costs prior to collecting from the parents. You receive orders from the parents and only those get printed. Proof programs eliminate the need to arrange a sales date in the school although your sales could benefit if you choose to set a sales date, meet with the parents and sell from the proofs.

A decided advantage of the proof program is that it allows you to offer a much wider variety of packaging options. In the speculative program you can only offer one, two or three different sheet options. With the proof program you are limited only by your imagination and the capability of your production lab.

There is a time penalty involved with the proof program. If you are having your proofs printed by your production lab, it will take the same amount of time to get them as it does to get finished prints. This can double your turn around time; the time from picture day until the parents have the finished product in hand.

Proof programs are not as effective at raising the sales average because they lack the impulse shopping factor. Also, parents are viewing small versions of their child's pictures and must use their imaginations to stretch these mini-images into full sized prints.

The proof forms must be attractive and offer a great deal of information about the program and its options without being cluttered. Payment methods have to be spelled out on the proof form and there should be a space for credit card purchasers to write in their account information.

Your proof form has to have complete contact information for your company, name, address, phone number and e-mail. You can expect to field several questions from the parents during a proof presentation.

I need to revisit one more aspect of the turn around time for proof programs. If you are having your proofs produced by a lab be sure to take into account any unusual time constraints, such as delivery before a major holiday, when choosing to use the proof program.

Finally, if you are using a proof program, be sure to tell the director how and when the finished prints will be delivered or shipped to her school for distribution to the parents.

A prepaid program will be your first choice if you are dealing with a school that provides bus service to transport all or most of the children to and from their homes. This arrangement is rare but it does exist. If you are dealing with such a school, and you fail to address it, you can lose your shirt.

The parents won't be coming to pick up children at a 'bussed' school and, therefore, won't be available to view pictures in a speculative program. A proof program is equally problematic as you will be depending on the the children to deliver your proofs to their parents. This is generally not an effective method to use.

The main thought behind a prepaid program is quite simply, 'no cash, no flash'. Its greatest drawback is that it generates the lowest dollar return of the three popular presentation methods.

Parents don't like to pay for something they can't see or touch. Also, you must rely on the school's director and staff to push your product when using the prepaid method.

The director will not spend much time building excitement for your product unless she is getting something significant in return. And so, not only are the expected revenues lower with prepaid, you will also have to share your profit with the school.

I have used a combination prepay, proof program that worked out well. It offers a standard, two pose, six sheet package for a prepaid cost equal to 50% of the regular price. On picture day all the chidren are photographed without regard to whether or not they have paid. On delivery day the finished packages are left for those who have paid and proof sheets are made, displaying the full, regular prices, for those who had not paid. The prepaids cover the cost of the shoot and yield a small profit, the proof sales are all gravy.

One of the advantages independent child care photographers enjoy over the public school companies is that we can offer significantly larger packages, through speculative sales, and rely on impulse shopping to pull the dollars for us. If we opt for prepaid programs, we are surrendering that advantage. Our packages will have to be similar in cost to those offered in the public school or they won't generate any response.

If you use prepaid programs, always include mail order forms when you deliver the orders. You already have the images and this is an opportunity to increase the individual order sizes. The mail order form should resemble your proof form. Having the image printed on this form will help you to identify the correct child, from your archives, when it comes time to fill the orders.

We are now printing our own proof forms in order to eliminate the added time at the lab. We print them on a good quality ink jet paper and, since the layout of form is stored in the computer, we need only insert the images as they are edited. We have used this system for one complete season, as of this writing, and it has worked very well.

And now to those necessary evils, commissions and spiffs. I offer a commission up front to the child care director whenever her help is essential to the success of the program. This is generally true with a prepaid program. Unless someone in the child care facility is pushing your product, you are winking in the dark. Your commission schedule should be based on a percentage of sales. The more successful the director is in selling your photography, the more she earns.

Commissions paid for speculative and proof programs are at your discretion or dictated by the market forces in your area. Don't be influenced by the commission rates paid in the public school market. While these can reach or exceed 40% of gross, they have no bearing on your business.

Commissions paid in child care photography rarely exceed 10% of the gross sales. The actual dollars amounts we pay to a typical child care facility are quite large when compared to their other fund raising activities.

Another way to approach the subject of commissions is to let the director know that your prices are skirting dangerously close to break even but that you will be only too happy to reprint your price lists, prior to the portrait sale date, to include any amount she might want for her school. This especially useful if the director is asking a higher than usual commission percentage.

"Freebies" are often used in lieu of a commission. Gift items, especially those that can be printed to incorporate the facility's name, can be used as an attractive alternative to cash commissions. Freebies are presented as a way of promoting good will between the school and its clients and, as you will point out, have a more lasting value.

One note of caution. Don't offer portrait sheets as "freebies" to the parents. The biggest sales tool you have going for you is the perceived value of the portraits. When you give any of them away for free, you are in effect lowering the perceived value of the ones you want to sell. The unspoken question in the parent's mind is, "if this one is free, why is this other one worth $15?"

The exception to this rule is classroom groups. If a director wants a commission and can be persuaded to accept classroom group pictures, for resale, in lieu of the commission, it's a win-win.

A 10% commission on a $40 sale is $4. Your production cost for a 5X7 classroom group will be well under a dollar. The director can sell the classroom 5X7 for $5 or more. She makes more and you pay a lot less.

Portrait gifts, such as calendars, coffee mugs, key chains, jig saw puzzles, tote bags and a host of other items are widely available at production labs, discount store photo departments, and on the web.

Do your homework to see if offering a freebie will save you money when done in lieu of commissions. The magic number is 5% of the full package asking price on a speculative program since that's what a 10% commission based on total gross will cost you.

Don't overlook the possibility of using these same gift items as the basis for fundraisers. Child care directors are always on the look out for opportunities to bring dollars into their activity funds.

Any item upon which children's pictures will be printed can be presented as a fundraiser. This gives the photographer another approach to selling the idea of photographing the children, as well as an opportunity to present portraits as an addition to the basic fundraiser, or as an after market item.

The number and variety of possible fund raisers that you, as a child care photographer, might want to add to your product mix would require a book of its own. I strongly urge you to do your homework in this area. The computer is your gateway to all the information you will need to make an informed choice and the time spent here will more than pay for itself by adding value to the products and services you offer.

Pricing the product is one of the most difficult tasks facing a photographer new to the child care market. If prices are too low, the photographer has a hard time maintaining profitability. If prices are too high, it's difficult to book schools. The key is to set prices that are 'just right'. The price for your portraits should be at or slightly above the average for child care photography in your area. The biggest problem you will face in setting prices within those parameters is that you don't know what the competition is charging. School photographers jealously guard their pricing information. But there is one place where they cannot keep their prices secret; the schools in which they have photographed.

An efficient booker is also somewhat of a detective. It is imperative, when calling on schools, to garner as much information about the competition as possible. This must be done in a conversational, matter of fact manner. Your booking presentation will be peppered with phrases like. “Oh, by the way.” and “So, that's what we do. How does that compare with....?”

The information about the competition, gleaned during the booking calls, will help to tailor your programs to fit the area standards. You will be better able to decide whether to meet or beat the others in pricing.

Price points are subject to change as the cost of doing business changes. This said, let's now explore some sample pricing guidelines to help get you started.

As previously noted, the simplest way to price your portraits is by the sheet. I prefer this method because it eliminates a lot of time wasted fielding questions about the make up of predetermined packages and what can or can not be substituted. A sheet is a sheet is a sheet.

The standard "sheet" is an 8X10. It can printed in several formats. As an example, an 8X10 sheet might have one 8X10 or, perhaps, 2 5X7's. It might be one 5X7 and 4 wallets or even a full sheet of wallets. Your production lab will be able to show you the full range of combinations available. For pricing purposes, a sheet is a sheet, no matter which combination of image sizes is printed on it. You don't own a pair of scissors and therefore can't cut the sheets. Often you will be asked to do so and your standard answer will be that your company's accounting is done by computer and the program does not allow for half sheets. Then apologize for the computer's shortcomings and sell the full sheet.

A typical 3 sheet per pose package, as presented by our company, will contain 1 8X10, 1 combination sheet (5X7, 2 3.5X5) and a sheet of all wallets, for each pose. Our 2 sheet per pose package contains 1 8X10 and one combination sheet (5X7, 3.5X5 and 2 wallets) for each pose.

Our current pricing starts with any single sheet for $15. A second, third and fourth sheet are added at $10. All subsequent sheets are priced at $5 each. A full 3 pose, 2 sheet per pose package sells for $55 plus local sales tax. Except for sheet number one, this pricing is slightly above average in our area.

It is important to keep the initial single sheet price relatively low as this helps the booker in handling price considerations. Directors will invariably ask how much the packages cost. The booker then explains that the pricing is by the sheet, but it starts at only $15 (or whatever you decide to set as your basic price) and the parents can buy as many or as few as they desire. In effect the booker is saying, "I can't tell you what the package costs because the parents are free to tailor whatever size package they want." That statement, coupled with a low initial sheet price, usually moves the presentation past the pricing stage.

Our chief competitor in this market, a giant in school photography, is a company that, due to economies of scale, can keep prices far below anything an independent photographer could ever match. Since we can't compete on price, we have to play to our strengths which are prompt responses to any request, individualized service and a total lack of bureaucracy. If a decision is needed, we can make it on the spot.

Reorders can add a significant cash flow to your child care photography business. There are several ways to address the handling of these reorders. The most lucrative method is to handle all aspects of the reorder business yourself. This approach requires that you be well organized to handle it. You have to know where you put things when you need to retrieve them weeks, months or even years later.

Fortunately the computer age has taken most of the sting out of the process of archiving your images. You need only divide each school into sub sets according to classrooms or age groups and burn them to a disc. Each disc is then titled with the school's name and the date shot. You merely file the discs by the month and year shot, and wait for the reorders to roll in.

The tedium sets in when you find that reorders don't come all neatly packaged, from one school at a time. They will arrive instead, at odd intervals, one at a time, from across the spectrum of the schools you have photographed. You must then recover that one image from your files, arrange to have it printed, and either mail it to the child care facility or to the parent's home address. Due to the extra work and expense involved in filling reorders, you should charge more for this service. We ask an additional $10, plus postage and handling (currently $2), on all reorders.

As an alternative, you can subscribe to an online fulfillment service for your reorder business. This requires that you upload images to the service and set your prices. They in turn handle all your reorder sales and remit your portion of the sales price to whatever bank account you have set up for that purpose.

Typically the fulfillment company will offer a wide range of portrait sizes, gift items and specialty items, such as portraits printed on stretched canvas, far exceeding anything you could offer from a home based photography business. They will quote a minimum price for each of their services and allow you to set your prices for whatever you feel traffic will bear, above those minimums.

A third option is to not involve yourself in reorders at all. The mechanism used to satisfy the parent while avoiding the reorder question all together is the 'copyright release'. You provide the parent, usually after they have purchased a specified minimum of your portraits, with a preprinted, signed document reassigning your copyright to them and granting any reproduction facility the right to copy those images.

This accomplishes two things: First of all it relieves you of any involvement in filling reorders and, secondly it gives you a lever to increase the average number of sheets being sold in the here and now.

When using the copyright release in lieu of reorders, we set the sales minimum to qualify at two or three sheets in a proof program whereas, in the case of speculative sales, they must purchase the full package available. For prepaid sales we do not offer a copyright release but do include a proof order form with each package delivered.

Another aspect of after market service is the guarantee. Our portraits carry a lifetime quality guarantee. If the image fades or discolors, we will replace it free of charge. They must, of course, return the original print at their own expense. The number of parents taking us up on this offer remains at zero while the advantage of having this as a selling point, during the booking call, places us head and shoulders above the competition.

The only down side is that you must be prepared to back up your guarantee if ever called upon to do so. Again, the computer comes to your rescue. If you are storing images for your reorder program, the same discs will be there in case someone exercises the guarantee. If you are not doing your own reorder fulfillment, the archives need not be complicated. Simply burn each school to its own disc and file it away. Chances that you will ever actually need the images in order to make good on a guarantee are slim to none.

The portrait delivery envelopes represent a golden opportunity for those photographers engaged in areas other than child care. If you are in this category, be sure include a list of all your services in each child care package. Without regard to which method of presenting the child care program is being used, you will have a final delivery envelope and it represents client contact with zero capture cost.

Generally speaking, amassing a client list is the biggest hurdle facing anyone who sells a service. Photographic services are no different. Early on we discussed how to find clients in the child care market. For those who are offer services in addition to child care photography, the schools provide an excellent method of reaching potential clients.

At some point in the picture sales process you will have the opportunity to gather names and addresses from the parents. You can have them fill out a simple form during a speculative sales presentation or, with proof orders, ask them to fill in the information blanks on the proof forms that are being returned to you.

Create a data bank for these clients and target seasonally appropriate direct mail advertising to them. You can always begin the initial mailing by thanking them for having purchased their child's portrait from you.

Plan to call back on each child care facility after your program has run its course. Call backs are usually the function of the booker. The purpose of the call back is to get a critique of the program in general and to deal with any problem areas that may have cropped up but were not mentioned by the director. Often a small discrepancy, too slight to mention at the time, will grow, in retrospect, into a major reason to not re-book with your company. It is important that you let the facility director know that you value her input, and that no concern is too small to be addressed.

If all went well and there are no problems to be resolved, rebook her. It is never too early to set an appointment for the following season or the following year.

Child care directors often follow their whims when it comes to ancillary services. The next 'pretty face', who walks into the school with the latest whiz-bang photography gimmick, could very well turn her head and cause you to lose a client. If she has already set a date with you, no matter how far in the future it may be, the chances are greatly reduced that the new guy will even be allowed to make a presentation.

Be sure to ask for referrals. Child care owners and directors have friends in the business and, if you have made a good impression, they will be happy to give you references.

## SECTION SEVEN ACTION CHECKLIST

1. LOCATE PACKAGE PROCESSING LABS IN YOUR AREA.
   a. TELEPHONE DIRECTORY.
   b. REFERRALS FROM OTHER PHOTOGRAPHERS.
   c. DISCOUNT AND WAREHOUSE SALES OUTLETS.

2. ASK TO SEE SAMPLES OF THEIR WORK.
   a. HAVE SOME OF YOUR OWN WORK PROCESSED.
   b. INCLUDE UNDER AND OVER EXPOSED IMAGES TO TEST HOW THE LAB HANDLES PROBLEMS.

3. DETERMINE WHICH SHEET COMBINATIONS ARE AVAILABLE.

4. NARROW YOUR SELECTION TO TWO LABS.
   a. SPLIT YOUR BUSINESS BETWEEN THEM UNTIL YOU HAVE A BASIS FOR FORMING A PREFERENCE.

5. GET TO KNOW THE PEOPLE WORKING AT THOSE LABS.

6. SET UP A FILE FOR ALL LAB CORRESPONDENCE.

7. OBTAIN OR CREATE LAB ORDER FORMS

8. GO ONLINE AND SEARCH OUT FULFILLMENT COMPANIES.

9. SET UP AN ACCOUNT WITH ONE OR MORE.

10. ASSEMBLE SPECULATIVE SALES MATERIALS.
    a. CASH BOX WITH SMALL BILLS AND CHANGE.
    b. CHARGE IMPRINTER OR READER.
    c. SMALL FOLDING TABLE.
    d. PRICE LISTS.
    e. BALL POINT PENS.
    f. COPYRIGHT RELEASES (OPTIONAL).
    g. PROOF FORMS FOR UNSOLDS.
    h. PORTRAIT DELIVERY ENVELOPES.
    i. RECEIPT PADS.

11. PROOF ORDER FORMS WITH DELIVERY ENVELOPES.

12. PREPAID PROGRAM FORMS WITH DELIVERY ENVELOPES.

13. CLASSROOM GROUP PICTURE ENVELOPES.

14. CONTACT URL FORMS FOR ONLINE SALES (OPTIONAL).

"if lost, claim that you're taking the scenic route."

# SECTION EIGHT

## FORMS AND RELATED MATERIAL

Child care photography, like any other business, requires you to keep track of, and to dispense, information by means of printed material. In order to fulfill this business requirement, you must either obtain or create the needed printed material. This section serves as a guide to such forms and related materials.

The child care photography business is divided into four distinct phases:

1. Booking
2. Photography
3. Sales
4. Reorders

'Booking' is the term applied to the activity of contacting child care facilities, describing the programs and setting a date for the photography to take place.

'Photography' refers to bringing a set of camera equipment into a school, setting up the equipment, capturing the images of the children, completing all follow up procedures, whether digital or film, and delivering the images to the processing lab.

'Sales' is any of the various processes involved in getting the finished portraits to the parents and collecting payment for them.

'Reorders' are any sales activities that take place after the initial portrait sales for a given school are concluded.

The following is a general list of forms needed to carry out these activities. It is not meant to be all inclusive. Each independent child photography company will vary in some way from others engaged in the business, and the forms used will also vary.

The forms listed below will serve as a starting point but you, the individual company operator, will make the final decision as to which forms and formats best suits your needs.

Please note that this list is not in any order of importance. Review the entire list prior to creating your forms or having them printed.

1. Contact Information Print Outs.
    a. Review section 2.
2. Agreement Forms.
    a. A simple form which spells out what is expected from the child care facility and from the photography company.
3. Prepayment Envelopes.
    a. Preprinted with space for the parent's name, the child's name and the photography date.
4. Prepayment Package Price List.
    a. To be enclosed in pre-payment envelope.
    b. Lists packages, prices and payment methods.

c. Should include space for credit card purchase information.

5. Sign Up Sheets.
    a. Any lined sheet of paper will do.
    b. Write or have preprinted “Sign Up Sheet” at top.
    c. Have all participating parents sign sheet for prepaid program. This sheet serves as a cross check in case child is to be photographed but forgets or loses prepay envelope.
    d. If speculative program, only those parents NOT wanting their children photographed should sign.
7. Portrait Day Posters.
    a. 11X17, printed black ink on bright colored stock.
    b. Pre printed with your company name and a request that children be colorfully dressed.
    c. Blank spaces to write in photography day, date and time.
    d. A space for a sample picture of a child taken on the same background to be used.
8. Portrait Return Date Posters.
    a. This is basically the same as above except it has 'Portraits Will Be Here' and a space to write in the day, date and time.
    b. The request that children be dressed colorfully is eliminated.
    c. It is advisable to have the second poster printed on a different color stock so that the change of is more noticeable to the parents.
9. Portrait Samples.
    a. Use your own if you have them.
    b. Create samples by photographing your own children or those of neighbors and friends.
    c. Some processing labs will furnish samples. Explore this only if you can’t create your own.
10. Gift Item Samples.

a. Have samples of any gift items or 'freebies' you intend to use and take them with you on all booking calls.

11. Proof Program Order Forms.
    a. Must have a space for samples of all poses offered.
    b. Includes a complete break down of prices.
    c. Has a space for parent's name and mailing address.
    d. Has a place to collect credit card sales information.
    e. Contains your company name and contact information.
    f. Can also serve as reorder forms with the addition of your late order fees and shipping and handling fees.
12. Date Logs.
    a. Use only one date log book per photographer.
    b. If the booker and photographer are not the same person, each should have their own date log.
    c. Date log entries are to be made in pencil because photography dates are subject to change.
13. Business Cards.
    a. Always carry a supply of your business cards.
14. Street Maps.
    a. Street finder books are the easiest to work with while in your vehicle.
    b. Your best source for street maps when working small towns will be either the local bank or the chamber of commerce.
15. Booking Calls List and Routing.
    a. Cultivate the habit of routing your calls in advance.
    b. Try to have at least one extra week's calls routed in case something happens that prevents you from routing for the following week.
16. Thank You Cards.

a. A simple "'hank you' to distribute to your clients.
b. Can be mailed or placed into portrait delivery envelopes.
c. Lists the other services you provide.
d. Contains contact information for your company.

17. Additional Equipment.
    a. Cash box or bank bag for making change at a sale.
    b. A charge imprinter or card reader. Keep in mind that you will not be able to use the school's land line for your card reader.
    c. A calculator.
    d. A portable table to use in your sales completion area.
    e. Storage containers for your archival school discs.
    f. Various boxes and storage bins to transport props, toys and assorted items to the schools.
    g. Copyright release forms.
18. A Smile. (Not a form, but nice to have.)

As stated above, this list is not meant to contain all of the forms and publications you will ever need to conduct your child care photography business. It is intended to give you a good starting point, one that will allow you to hit the ground running when you take that plunge into the industry.

As you progress in the business, you will undoubtedly create new and better forms for your own usage but those listed above will get you started in the right direction.

## SECTION EIGHT ACTION CHECKLIST

1. REVIEW THIS SECTION AND CREATE A SEPARATE CHECKLIST OF THE FORMS YOU WILL BE NEEDING.

2. CHECK WITH YOUR PROCESSING LAB TO SEE WHICH FORMS THEY MAY REQUIRE WITH YOUR IMAGES.

3. USING THE SAMPLES PROVIDED, DESIGN YOUR OWN FORMS TO MEET THE GUIDELINES OUTLINED IN THIS SECTION.

4. DIVIDE THE FORMS INTO GROUPS FOR EACH OF THE FOUR BUSINESS ACTIVITIES.

5. TEACH YOUR CO WORKERS HOW TO USE THE FORMS PROPERLY.

6. CREATE SIMPLE SEQUENCE OF ACTIVITY CHECKLISTS FOR EACH PHASE OF THE BUSINESS AND USE THEM WHEN TRAINING YOUR CO-WORKERS.

"never let yesterday take up too much of today"

## SECTION NINE

## ADDING TO YOUR STAFF

As your business grows, you will eventually reach a point at which you can no longer handle all its various aspects single handed. The time will come when you will find it necessary to invite someone into your circle of enterprise. There are no hard, fast rules for determining when this point has been reached. You will know that you are there when you start feeling as though you are riding a rodeo bull, and every time the clock reaches seven and a half seconds, someone resets it.

By using the appropriate programs and given sufficient dedication to purpose, a single person can book, shoot and sell up to three schools per week. I would personally consider this level of activity to be a job and a half but It can be done by one if the sales are either prepaid or proof programs.

Typically you would be shooting Tuesday, Wednesday and Thursday while making all the booking calls on Monday and Friday. Your sales programs would have to be proof or pre pay since this schedule would not leave time for you to keep up with editing, paperwork, and associated errands, and still be available to offer a speculative sales program three evenings per week.

When you have made the decision that it is time to expand, you will be faced with another, equally important choice. You will have to decide which phase or phases of the business you want to do personally, and which will be offered as a job opportunity.

How successfully you screen and select employees will determine whether or not your business continues to grow and prosper.

There are several approaches open to you for recruiting potential employees. The first, and most obvious, is to place ads in the local newspapers. Your newspaper ads will contain a brief description of what the job entails, and a means for the applicants to contact you. The number of applicants you receive will depend in large part on the job market in your area but, no matter how many responses you get, you will have to answer each of them.

I would advise that you set up a method of receiving the applicant responses that does not involve you having to personally answer the phone and field their initial questions. This may be accomplished by publishing a phone number that goes directly to a message machine, by enlisting the services of an office suites answering service, or by simply asking that written replies be sent to your business address.

You can also conduct your applicant search by word of mouth, soliciting potential employees through friends or business contacts, or by contacting local community colleges and tech schools.

Most office supply stores will stock generic employee application forms. Either purchase a book of these, or simply design your own.

You will want a completed application and a current resume, or other job history outline, from each applicant.

There are privacy issues to consider when asking someone to fill out a job application. The time to address this concern is before you allow an applicant to enter any personal information on the form you have provided. When handing them the form simply say something like, "If there is any question on this form that you would not feel comfortable answering, leave it blank. It will not be held against you in the interview process."

The decision as to which aspect of the business you will want to hire someone for is highly personal and will depend, in great measure, on which parts of the business you would prefer to handle yourself. We will discuss the requirements for each position, keeping in mind that you may very well be hiring someone to perform two or more functions.

The chief requirement for a child care photographer is the ability to work with children. You will never hear anyone admit, during the interview phase of the hiring process, that they can't work with children. If the person you are considering lacks direct experience working with the child care age group, you must expose them to the child care environment and see first hand how they react. There is no other practical way to assess how they will interact with children.

The most efficient way to accomplish this is to simply have the applicant drop by a school where you are photographing. This process may have to be spread over several days if you have more than one applicant. Always get clearance from the school director prior to asking an applicant to meet you at a child care facility.

Make the applicant feel a part of the proceedings. Explain what you are doing, and why you are doing it, as the photography session unfolds.

Observe him or her as the children enter and exit. Be alert for verbal clues as to how they feel about the children, especially the occasional difficult child.

Our personal prejudices will always be a factor when we interview and hire. This is especially true when the company is our own “baby.”

When it comes to filling a child care photography position, I tend to favor female photographers, between the ages of 25 and 35. This is 'mom’s age'; the age and gender most familiar to the children being photographed and, therefore, usually well within their comfort zone. This said, I have hired and successfully trained photographers, male and female, who ranged in age from 19 to 63.

The point is that you will bring preconceived notions to the hiring process, and that is to be expected. But don’t let them blind you to the excellent applicant who falls outside those parameters.

If you are interviewing candidates for the booker’s position a whole different set of priorities comes into play. The booker’s job calls for a more mature approach than does that of the photographer.

The booker is usually the first person from your company to contact a child care director. They are the face of your company, so to speak. You want someone who dresses well, has a good command of the language, and reacts quickly to oral responses in conversation.

Your representative may well be one of a very few adult contacts, other than school employees, that the director will have during her work day. Most child care directors, unless they are truly busy with some project, welcome the opportunity to speak to someone on an adult level.

The person you hire to make booking calls has to be comfortable with the idea of cold calls and not afraid of the word "no." He or she must realize that sales is a game of averages and that not every call will result in a closed deal. Quite the opposite is true. The 'booked' school is a pleasant break in a stream of calls that do not result in bookings. Your booker must have the attitude that each "no" merely brings him or her a step closer to the next "yes."

Just as with the photographer, the potential booker needs to be exposed to field conditions. Child care photography is a unique business genre. You can't toss a stone in an average crowd and have it land on someone experienced in this business. Your applicants, hearing the child care photography job description, will consider it 'a piece of cake.' After all, how hard can it be to work with kids or to get someone to agree to have children photographed?

But the reality is that the person you are considering probably has never done anything remotely resembling what you will be requiring of them.

It is only fair to the applicant that they be afforded the opportunity to experience the job, in the field, prior to agreeing to sign on. It is equally important for you to be able to observe them under fire before you make the offer.

As a small business owner you will have some disadvantages when compared to the mega-photography companies. You can't offer the perks, the profit sharing, retirement plans and other inducements the big guys use to attract employees. This does not mean that you won't be able to hire and keep top notch people. It merely means that you have to play to your strengths.

You are small, but you are caring. You are "family." Your employees are not just tiny cogs in a gigantic machine. Far from that, they are trusted, valued, needed and appreciated.

You have the opportunity to share the joy of building a new business from the ground up. Use this excitement, pay fair wages, treat your employees the way you want to be treated and you'll have no problem in attracting people with whom you will want to share your business life.

Experience is desirable, but usually brings some baggage with it. When interviewing experienced candidates, you must determine if they are capable of 'unlearning' past methods of operation that might get in the way of doing business your way.

Always be mindful that, whenever you send someone into a child care facility, photographer, booker or portrait sales person, you are entrusting your good name and reputation to that person. It is imperative that you exercise caution when selecting someone to represent you to your clients.

You need to know why they left their last position. Always check references. In today's business climate it is difficult to get a straight answer when calling for references so be alert for subtleties.

Do not rush through the hiring process. Child care photography is a seasonal business which allows the opportunity for you to anticipate future hiring needs. Set up interviews in advance of the next busy season and allow time to complete your due diligence before you actually need boots on the ground.

There are several categories to consider when adding people to your organization. You might be bringing on 'employees' or, perhaps, 'independent contractors' or even 'partners'. Each designation has a specific legal definition and your level of responsibility changes depending on which category is applicable.

Do not fly blindly in this area. Talk to someone who can give you specific answers for your specific situation. Your CPA, the IRS, SCORE, your banker, the Small Business Administration, are all excellent sources of information and this question should be resolved as soon as you decide to add staff but prior to placing any ads or conducting interviews.

The next subject to cover is that of compensation. No matter how nice a boss you are, they will probably not work for free. How and what to pay your employees is entirely up to you, so long as you comply with any federal and local laws that might apply in your area. I will share with you what we are doing in our business but this information is strictly for illustrative purposes. It is not a 'one size fits all' pay plan. Feel free to try it if you think it will suit your needs. If not, by all means investigate what other companies are doing and adapt some of their methods to your company.

We set 35% of gross income as our in-house labor cost. The owner's pay is included in that percentage and is determined by which slots we personally fill.

The breakdown is as follows:

a. Bookers 10%
b. Photographers 15%

c. Portrait Sales 10%

A portrait sales position is not needed unless you are using a speculative sales program. Prepaid and proof programs fall under administrative duties and we usually handle those without involving employees.

When we present a speculative program, we handle the sales duties alone or with the help of our booker and/or photographer. The size of the sales staff needed is dictated by the number of portrait packages to be presented. When added help is required, the 10% sales payroll is split evenly among the sales crew.

As you progress in this business you will establish averages. Your booking will reach a point of predictability expressed as a ratio of signed bookings to calls made and your sales will likewise be expressed in average sales per child (package) photographed.

Soon these numbers will dominate your future planning. You will, for instance, find yourself asking "how many packages do I need to pay for that new camera." Your booker should be encouraged to also think along these lines as it directly links the number of bookings, which are a factor of calls made, to his or her desired income level.

The photographer is pretty much at the mercy of the booker as far as volume is concerned but he or she controls sales averages by the quality of the work produced.

Don't keep your people in the dark. Use the images you are selling to the parents as examples when you discuss the state of the business with your staff. Show them the product and get their opinions on how it might be improved.

Talk to them about sales averages and the bookings-to-calls-made ratios. Let them know that they are directly responsible the company's profits or losses and, since they are paid on a percentage basis, also responsible for their own level of income.

Above all, your staff will want to feel that they are a part of the company and that their input is valuable to you.

## SECTION NINE ACTION CHECKLIST

1. DECIDE WHETHER OR NOT YOU NEED TO ADD STAFF.

2. DETERMINE WHICH POSITION YOU WANT TO HIRE OUT.
   a. REPLACING YOURSELF AS PHOTOGRAPHER LEAVES YOU WITH MORE MOBILITY THAN DOES REPLACING YOURSELF AS BOOKER.

3. PLACE CLASSIFIED ADS IN THE NEWSPAPER.

4. CONTACT COMMUNITY COLLEGE OR TECH SCHOOLS.

5. ARRANGE TO RECEIVE AD RESPONSES.

6. CALL EACH APPLICANT TO VERIFY MAILING ADDRESSES.

7. MAIL APPLICATIONS AND REQUESTS FOR RESUMES.

8. SCREEN RESPONSES AND CHECK REFERENCES.

9. SCHEDULE INTERVIEWS.
   a. RENT A HOTEL MEETING ROOM IF YOU LACK OFFICES.
   b. SCHEDULE INTERVIEWS AT REGULAR INTERVALS.
   c. DISCUSS ALL ASPECTS OF THE POSITION, ESPECIALLY INCOME POTENTIAL.

10. NARROW YOUR FILED OF APPLICANTS TO THE BEST TWO OR THREE.
    a. SCHEDULE THEM, ONE AT A TIME, FOR AN OBSERVATION FIELD TRIP WITH YOU.

11. MAKE A FINAL SELECTION AND SCHEDULE TRAINING.

12. SEEK PROFESSIONAL ADVICE CONCERNING ANY LEGALITIES PRIOR TO ACTUALLY INTERVIEWING OR HIRING ANYONE.

“do not muzzle the ox that treads the grain"

## SECTION TEN

## OVERVIEW

Child care photography falls into that broad category of things that are simple, but not necessarily easy. The concept is extremely simple. You book them, you shoot them and then you sell the images.

Execution of the concept, however, takes a bit of effort.

To be successful in this business you have to be a self-starter and you must associate yourself with others who are also self-starters. Each phase of the operation is totally dependent on all the other phases, each person in your organization must be capable of working without direct supervision.

As stated earlier, it is not necessary to reinvent the wheel when you embark on your child care photography career. The concept has been proven many times over. The greatest obstacle to overcome is the idea that you must be a giant, nationwide operation in order to succeed in this business. Nothing could be further from the truth. In fact, the business climate actually favors the mom and pop approach. What you surrender in economies of scale are more than compensated for by your ability to react quickly to local market forces, and to make decisions absent an entrenched bureaucracy.

I will be first to admit that there is a certain advantage to being an employee of a major child care photography company when starting out in the industry. I was fortunate enough to stumble into this field while actually looking for something else to do. I was trained by one of the best in the business and had no worries about losing investment capital should the whole thing not work out.

But not everyone can enter into the child care photography profession as an employee of a major company. The number of people who make their living in this fashion is actually rather small. When you consider that there are only a half dozen or so companies offering child care photography on a national scale and that they, on average , employ no more than a couple hundred photographers each, that comes to a fairly small number compared to the general population.

Child care photographers belong to a fairly small club, and there is plenty of room for more players.

As far as an initial investment is concerned, it is actually possible, more so than in other industries, to enter into this business on the tiniest of shoestrings. We have discussed at length what it takes to enter into the business and hit the ground running. Now let's consider what your approach might be if you want to be in the child care photography business but can't afford to purchase the full set of required equipment.

What would you say if I told you that all you needed by was a good digital camera and a willingness to put yourself out there? Just that? Period?

Here's how it can be done. You follow all the advice in sections one, two and three but when you call on the schools to book them you present only programs that can be handled with a single, hand held camera. The obvious choice is class room groups. They can be taken outdoors or, if inside, with a good, camera mounted strobe.

You can also build simple fund raising programs around any of several concepts available to you by partnering with companies that are in the fund raising business. The key, of course, is to select those offering programs that require only simple images from you.

This approach to the business will allow you to begin a revenue stream, purchase equipment with the profits, and be ready to book your full program for the following year

That's it. The preceding nine sections contain pretty much all that I can put in a simple 'how to' manual. It would be impossible to give you a blow by blow account of over a quarter century in the business. The best I can say on that score is, "Hey, you had to be there."

The world has totally changed since I ventured into that first child care facility so many years ago. I still remember my first school. It was named "Esperanza", the Spanish word for "hope." And hope was the primary thing I had going for me that day.

The camera was an old Camerz Classic twin lens loaded with 100 feet of 35MM film. The Photogenic power pack and lights were obsolete, even by the standards of the day, but they worked. I had hired on with a nationally known child photography company whose philosophy was to give the new guys old equipment to learn on before trusting them with state-of-the-art gear. Although they had a training program that was truly comprehensive, it didn't include a section on how to wrangle the butterflies in the belly, the first time you set up in a school all on you own.

It was scary but, when a staff person brought the first group of kids into the room, everything changed. I learned a lesson that no training instructor had ever mentioned. I learned that I was wearing the "mantle of authority."

Allow me to digress by way of explanation. If you are in a fast food restaurant, you reasonably expect the young lady behind the counter, the one wearing the uniform of the establishment, to be able to answer any question that you might have about the menu items or prices in that restaurant. Your expectation does not take into account that she might be a new hire, her first time on the counter, and less knowledgeable about the product mix than you, the customer. You expect her to have a certain level of knowledge because of where she is standing and what she is wearing. She has on the "mantle of authority."

Standing in the child care facility, that morning so long ago, it dawned on me that I was the only one in the room who was expected to know what happens next and, no matter what I did it would be the right thing to do because I was wearing the 'mantle of authority'.

When you make your first booking call you will be representing a major child care photography firm. Your own. You will be the expert in what you do. If you believe in yourself and believe in your product, you will not be able to say or do a wrong thing. That's just the way it works.

As a photographer, if you can throw off your adult inhibitions and act childlike for a few hours at a stretch, you will succeed. All the rest is purely mechanics.

Someone, wiser than me, once said that the test for your ideal occupation is to consider what you would busy yourself with if all your needs were met and income was not a factor. For me, child care photography has come mighty close.

The ball is now in your court. You have demonstrated an interest pursuing a career in child care photography by purchasing this manual but reading alone won't get it done. Now it's time for doing.

Start with section one. Complete the action checklist, taking notes as you go. If the manner in which the material is presented makes sense, then do it. If a next step raises questions, stop and consider where to go to get the answers. Once you put the process in motion, continue moving forward until you have accomplished the goal.

Random samples of the work we at Blue Sky Photography have done over the past few years are to be found at:

http://www.viewyourphoto.com/childcare

They have been posted as an adjunct to this manual, in the hope that they will illustrate a few of the possible poses and themes available to you. We welcome your comments and questions.

The smiles are all out there, waiting for you.

## SECTION TEN ACTION CHECKLIST

1. DO IT.

“there are a thousand reasons for failure
but not a single excuse”

Thank you for purchasing this manual.

It was written in the true belief that anyone who desires to do so can succeed in the child care photography business.

I realize that there will be unanswered questions as well as differences of opinion that arise from the material that I have presented and I welcome your questions and input.

Whether you wish to toss bouquets or brickbats, you can reach me via e-mail at

rixfoto@aol.com

or by mail

Blue Sky Studios
PO Box 1568
Magnolia, Texas, 77353

www.ingramcontent.com/pod-product-compliance
Ingram Content Group UK Ltd.
Pitfield, Milton Keynes, MK11 3LW, UK
UKHW051138260726
13967UKWH00010B/3116